▶ Sexuality and Globalization

Recovering Political Philosophy

Series Editors: **Thomas L. Pangle** and **Timothy W. Burns**

Titles include:

John Colman
LUCRETIUS AS THEORIST OF POLITICAL LIFE

Timothy Burns
SHAKESPEARE'S POLITICAL WISDOM

Thomas L. Pangle and J. Harvey Lomax (*editors*)
POLITICAL PHILOSOPHY CROSS-EXAMINED: PERENNIAL CHALLENGES TO THE PHILOSOPHIC LIFE

David Levy
EROS AND SOCRATIC POLITICAL PHILOSOPHY

Martin D. Yaffe and Richard S. Ruderman (*editors*)
REORIENTATION: LEO STRAUSS IN THE 1930s

Eric Buzzetti
XENOPHON THE SOCRATIC PRINCE: THE ARGUMENT OF THE ANABASIS OF CYRUS

Lee Ward
MODERN DEMOCRACY AND THE THEOLOGICAL-POLITICAL PROBLEM IN SPINOZA, ROUSSEAU, AND JEFFERSON

Laurent Bibard – translated by Christopher Edwards
SEXUALITY AND GLOBALIZATION: AN INTRODUCTION TO A PHENOMENOLOGY OF SEXUALITIES

NOT ADDED BY
UNIVERSITY OF MICHIGAN

palgrave▸pivot

Sexuality and Globalization: An Introduction to a Phenomenology of Sexualities

Laurent Bibard

Translated by
Christopher Edwards

palgrave
macmillan

SEXUALITY AND GLOBALIZATION
Copyright © Laurent Bibard, 2014.
All rights reserved.

First published in 2014 by
PALGRAVE MACMILLAN®
in the United States— a division of St. Martin's Press LLC,
175 Fifth Avenue, New York, NY10010.

Where this book is distributed in the UK, Europe and the rest of the world, this is by Palgrave Macmillan, a division of Macmillan Publishers Limited, registered in England, company number 785998, of Houndmills, Basingstoke, Hampshire RG216XS.

Palgrave Macmillan is the global academic imprint of the above companies and has companies and representatives throughout the world.

Palgrave® and Macmillan® are registered trademarks in the United States, the United Kingdom, Europe and other countries.

ISBN: 978-1-137-46926-7 EPUB
ISBN: 978-1-137-46929-8 PDF
ISBN: 978-1-137-47525-1 Hardback

Library of Congress Cataloging-in-Publication Data is available from the Library of Congress.

A catalogue record of the book is available from the British Library.

First edition: 2014

www.palgrave.com/pivot

DOI: 10.1057/9781137469298

Contents

Preface	vi
Acknowledgments	viii
Introduction	1
Part I Modernity	**5**
1 Appraisal	6
2 Insurrection	10
3 Christianity, Paganism, Judaism: The Fury of Practice	21
Part II The Sexes	**37**
4 Fractal Morals	39
5 Interlacings	46
6 Drama	57
Part III Time	**68**
7 On Methodology	69
8 Contradictions: Lives, Decisions, Thoughts	79
9 Love as a Responsible Presence	89
Bibliography	96
Index	98

Preface

Continental philosophy has yet to grapple seriously with human sexuality. The in-vogue discipline of gender studies has not bridged this gap. It is inevitable that studies emerge which aim to counterbalance the archaic male domination of the female. These studies are, however, insufficient in helping us understand the archaic origin of human sexuality and the role it plays in shaping us. *Sexuality and Globalization* is a tentative approach to this topic and related issues. The book's approach is to consider the human body as archaic, independent of any deliberate human will, and yet part of our effort to make sense of ourselves.

Increasingly, and especially since Heidegger, philosophy has been deconstructing its own bases and discovering a kind of a "naïveté" rooted in the initial effort to elaborate an ontological understanding of the whole. Such an ongoing deconstruction made possible the realization that the effort to think sexuality had yet to be seriously undertaken. The necessity of doing so was clear to me while writing *La sagesseet le feminin*'on Alexandre Kojève and Leo Strauss' discussion on tyranny (*On Tyranny* by Leo Strauss, including "Tyranny and Wisdom" by Alexandre Kojève, University of Chicago Press, 1961, 1991, 2000). I demonstrate, in *Wisdom and Feminity*, the extent to which the core issue of politics is located in Kojève and Strauss' points of view on sexuality. In other words, gender relations represent the foundation for understanding human political life.

Interestingly enough, Kojève and Strauss, despite their exchange on the subject of politics, fundamentally disagree on how to interpret the whole. For Kojève, History plays the role of an ontological repairing of the initially and apparently indomitable difference if not conflict between action and thought. For Strauss, this difference, if not conflict, is ontological and cannot be overcome. My analysis of Kojève and Strauss'works led me to the assumption that the "tension" between action and thought is analogous to a tension between the sexes. In other words, Kojève and Strauss' disagreement was to be interpreted as a disagreement concerning their understandings of gender relations.

I clarified my stance on Kojève in the presentation I published on one of Kojève's short essays on atheism (*L'athéisme*, Gallimard, 1998). The equivalent concerning Strauss is presented in—and to a certain extent, *as*—the second part of *Wisdom and Feminity* in which I analyze Strauss' comments on both Aristophanes' and some of Xenophon's works (naturally and especially *Oeconomicus*).

Sexuality and Globalization represents the deepening of my understanding of the crucial role of sexuality when it comes to understanding humans and human history, and the "world we live in" as Kojève would have put. Though rooted in the above-mentioned exchange between Kojève and Strauss about the whole, this book is not an analysis of their work. Rather it represents my effort to approach reality as such. Such an understanding implicates not only philosophy as a tentative understanding of the whole and a correlated way of life, but also religions as well, including the recent modern sciences and technologies. In line with some efforts of both modern and so-called post-modern philosophy, this book deals with the frontier between philosophy and what philosophy is not—as well as between what is not philosophy and philosophy. One of the consequences of such a tentative effort to ponder the whole, including the ontological possibility of being indifferent to questions concerning a possible understanding of the whole, is a certain way of writing which tries to stand between philosophy and literature. I apologize in advance if this effort did not result in an easy way to read this book.

Last but not least, *Sexuality and Globalization* is a shorter version of the considerably longer *Phenomenology of Sexualities*, to be published in the near future in France as *Phénoménologie des sexualités*. In other words, the present book represents the tipping point between a questioning about politics and a presentation of my understanding of reality as such. It is my hope that this tipping point makes sense in the context of globalization today, where gender relations represent and illustrate the most fundamental changes and stakes for humans' future.

Acknowledgments

Before leaving you to the text, I would like to thank Christopher Edwards, whose relentless efforts to understand every single word and wording of the French version of this book made possible the current publication in English. Without his exceptional perseverance, thoroughness and academic rigor, this publication would not have come to fruition.

I would like to especially thank my colleagues Thomas Pangle and Timothy Burns for their confidence in and support for this publication. I met Thomas in the early 1990s, together with some other alumni of Leo Strauss such as Nathan Tarcov and Clifford Orwin. It was with their help that I discovered Kojève and Strauss' works. I would like to thank Pierre Manent and Terence Marshall for introducing me to all these people as well as for facilitating my American networking.

I could havenever made any progress in my research and understanding of humans' reality which was the outcome of the many fruitful discussions about the whole that I had with these colleagues. I am grateful to Bernard Bourgeois, who has continuously supported my tentative philosophical understanding of reality. I would also like to thank my colleagues at ESSEC, particularly Laurent Alfandari, Marie-Laure Djelic, Alan Jenkins, Nicolas Mottis and RaduVranceanu, who trusted me and supported me in my research and academic endeavors. Many thanks to my students, who constantly asked relevant questions and raised relevant problems about the understanding of the whole, despite studying in a business school, where such a questioning and effort to approach reality on the basis of a genuine taste for understanding is not supposed to be relevant!

Last but not least, I am grateful to my friends and especially to my wife, Claire, who always accompanies me in my research—which she knows is not only an academic one but is also a quest for wisdom, or about making sense of life and reality. I could never make sense of life without her presence, enthusiasm and support.

Note

1   (L'Harmattan 2005); the title of this book that is yet to be published in English in the United States is *English Wisdom and Feminity*.

palgrave▶pivot

www.palgrave.com/pivot

Introduction

Abstract: *In this day and age sexuality is a central concern not only in defending women's rights but especially in people's everyday personal lives. It is essential in many ways, perhaps most significantly in the stability it brings to the lives of both men and women.*

The first observation of this essay is that the essential role sexuality plays in people's lives is very often disregarded. This disservice is rooted, as is the case for other concerns related to that which is tangible, in the perception of the body as a means for the desires born of consciousness and of a calculating and rational will that is both efficient and reliable.

Bibard, Laurent. *Sexuality and Globalization: An Introduction to a Phenomenology of Sexualities.*
New York: Palgrave Macmillan, 2014.
DOI: 10.1057/9781137469298.0004.

> "Love will no longer simply be a question of man and woman, but rather that of two humanities... two solitary beings protecting one another, complementing one another, stopping and bowing down before one another."
>
> Rainer Maria Rilke, Lettres à un jeune poète

In this day and age, sexuality is a central concern not only in defending women's rights but also in people's everyday personal lives. It is essential in many ways, perhaps most significantly in the stability it brings to the lives of both men and women.

The first observation of this essay is that the essential role sexuality plays in people's lives is very often disregarded. This disservice is rooted, as is the case for other concerns related to that which is tangible, in the perception of the body as a means for the desires born of consciousness and of a calculating and rational will that is both efficient and reliable.

Our world maintains a predatory rapport with nature, boundlessly enslaving all that appears to give itself naturally to possession and control. This un-nuanced statement is clearly both partial and unilateral: many believe that nature is no more governable than the body or even human sexuality. Successive efforts to "tune into the body" as if it were a language, and the growing success of trends that highlight the importance of a renewed interest in listening to nature and to the body are evidence of the values held by a not insignificant number of people who do not embrace a mechanical and predatory rapport with the tangible world in general and the body in particular. The fact remains that the first of the aforementioned observations stands in clear opposition to the second just as much as the latter is essential to the former. The discourse and lifestyles that enslave both the body and sexuality are thus juxtaposed against those who seek to liberate and listen to it.

* * *

Despite the strong bond that links them, it is still rare to associate globalization with the evolving relationship between humans and their sexuality. The second observation of this essay is that globalization is largely a result of a Renaissance-era decision to master "nature" and ultimately sexuality. The basis of this control is a singular and unique "virilization" that impedes the coexistence of the masculine and feminine that, while not always harmoniously so, have until now proven a fecund duo.

More precisely, for the purposes of this essay, globalization is understood as a tension between desiring to master nature and yielding to its indomitable nature. This desire, whose 17th-century meaning has been more or less passed down, is in fact eminently modern in comparison to the primarily ancient acceptance of non-mastery. In other words, globalization should be seen as the repetitive playing out of the tension between the modern desire for control and the ancestral acknowledgement of nature's uncontrollable quality rather than a ubiquitous extension of a homogenous and singular way of mastering nature.

In etymological terms, that which is "natural" occurs extempore, from within, rather than premeditatedly. Being extempore means not resulting from a meditated and deliberate desire to create something or someone, or a desire to have something made by something or someone else. In its essence sexuality symbolizes, in one way or another, what remains of extemporaneousness, even if the latter is losing ground to the spectacular progress being made in the domains of biotechnology and genetics.

At the heart of the battle between mastery (modern notion), and non-mastery or open-mindedness (ancient notion), sexuality is preparing itself as a test, realm and issue that is alternately free and captive, fueled by its own dynamism, and understood as a vector of man and woman's will. Questioning sexuality and the way in which it is experienced is a necessary step in finding, or perhaps rediscovering a meaning of life within globalization. Taking this step, on either side of the concurrently masculine and feminine, contemporary "virility," implies understanding the essence of these two sexualities and their relative worth prior to their metamorphosis by a transformative phenomenon that, driven by a desire for control, would redefine both. The "ancients" likely understood certain aspects of the masculine and feminine better than we: in this essay we are attempting to unravel their extemporaneous dynamic.

This book consists of three Parts:

> Assuming that economics is paramount in contemporary life, we will begin, in Part I, *Modernity*, by seeking the Western origins of globalization. This genealogy will lead us to ponder the respective roles played by paganism (of Greek origin in the West), Judaism, and Christianity. In Part II, *Sexes*, we will question the relationship between virility, the feminine and the masculine. This second step will logically begin by analyzing contemporary political trends with regard to sexuality. A phenomenology of the feminine and the masculine will follow and lead to a new understanding

of social, cultural and political questions in the contemporary sphere. In Part III, *Time*, we will focus on time as a privileged realm for the questions hereto articulated. This deliberation will be constituted by (1) the methodological approach of this essay, (2) the phenomenology of sexualities as a function of their relationship to time and, finally (3) the discerning, on an individual and collective level, of certain ethical, theoretical and practical outcomes of the former.

This essay calls upon a number of controversial events and points of view. As unconventional as the essay may be, reading it requires taking time to wander through the text and to venture into new ideas.

In any case, a precipitous reading is ill advised: we wish our readers a fruitful reading.

Part I
Modernity

1
Appraisal

Abstract: *This chapter makes clear some dominant aspects of current economic life and its social as well as psychological consequences: people participate in and benefit from, but at the same time are victims of, the current worldwide economy, which results in people lacking time. People lack time for everything. Particularly due to the exceptionally competitive economy, they are scared about the future. The question must be asked: why are people so deeply embedded in a global and dominant economy, without being able to get rid of its constraints and increasing looming dangers? This is to be answered in Chapter 2.*

Keywords: *dependency; economy; fear; global world*

Bibard, Laurent. *Sexuality and Globalization: An Introduction to a Phenomenology of Sexualities.*
New York: Palgrave Macmillan, 2014.
DOI: 10.1057/9781137469298.0006.

One identifiable constant of the world in which we live is the significance of the economy as a theoretical model, as a daily reality, as well as an authority imposing limits on people's personal and professional choices. The economy's stranglehold on the latter is engendered by the dominance of economic thought in political reasoning: there is a direct relationship between the power and influence of the State and the economic power that the latter is able to harness. An economy's strength is measured by its means: money. Be it by free will or by obligation, we all find ourselves faced with the choice of earning a living or, on an individual or national level, leading a marginalized existence. Money is not, however, the only means of an economic system. Making it ever more powerful are the technical advances that we continually make by mobilizing our collective imagination and knowledge. The sciences acquiesce to our ever-growing desire for knowledge and industrial capability. In fact, the only archaic aspect of our naming of the "military-industrial complex" as a coupling of war and money is its differentiation amongst other systems assumed to fall outside of its scope: the military-industrial complex *defines* the global economy in which we live, a world where everything is sooner or later either war-driven or strategic, economic or commercial, social albeit financial, and scientific or technological. The modern supremacy of the economy over other ways of living (religious, moral, political, philosophical, artistic, leisurely) boils down to the increasingly predictable struggle of man versus man in which each actor leverages his mastery of technical and/or financial prowess to his or his community's advantage.

Preparing oneself for life is thus tantamount to arming oneself for battle: understanding the world, contemplating its potential beauty, and being happy are no longer sufficiently convincing nor attainable objectives. Education is synonymous with amassing the knowledge requisite to finding one's place in an increasingly tumultuous world. Studying for the sake of intellectual prestige and knowledge or for the simple pleasure of doing so is no longer in vogue. Subsistence trumps the rest and because life is a game of survival of the fittest, having the means to do so is essential no matter the cost. The modern learner will only see the value of learning theory insofar as doing so will prepare him for an economic struggle that consists of augmenting his value on the job market. He would learn, for example, Heisenberg's theory of indetermination in quantum physics, perhaps only acquiring an elementary understanding of its fundamental elements, not for the sake of learning and understanding but rather for improving his chances of finding employment later in time. In today's world, man is primarily motivated by his fear for survival: regardless of the earner's social and cultural status, survival can be guaranteed only by finding work which will pay a monthly salary that allows for his continued existence. Fear undoubtedly operates continually on a feedback cycle by sustaining its own source. Fearing the powers of the economic sector bestows indomitable credibility upon them and the world that they symbolize. Such power is possible only if the participants in the economy's public and private sectors are themselves fearful puppets of the system upon which they seemingly depend. The degree to which the economy holds sway over man's life, regardless of whether he reaps profit from it or suffers from the relative constraints it imposes upon him, is directly, though not singularly, correlated to his fear of the system that he perpetuates.

Our world is notably characterized by the universal yet unmentionable sway that fear holds over each and every person reaching into the highest administrative, political, intellectual, economic, and financial stratospheres.

The growing degree of complexity and uncertainty (the first of which is partially responsible for the second) that characterizes human life feeds fear on all levels. Relationships, exchanges, and interdependencies amongst individuals, societies, cultures, businesses, and States are such that the analytical approaches to their relative processes are ineffective. "Complex thought," in other words trusting one's fallible intuition, is the only strategy capable of providing an absolute or holistic approach to the world. The word "approach," as opposed to fixed definitions and knowledge of objects, is key for the ultimate goal is efficient, real-time decision-making, or, in other words, rushed decision-making. Since time is a commodity, meticulously examining every question is an inefficient strategy. As a result decision-makers merely skim over important matters, pondering them at best, ignoring them at worst. Thus, the constraints imposed by the contemporary world and its economy lead to a fundamental fear of not knowing how to be relevant in today's world as well as utter uncertainty with regard to rushed decision-making resulting from the complexity of the questions at hand. Such an appraisal of human life contributes to a defining tension of our era: fear feeds the desire to establish oneself with certainty and reassurance with regard to decisions made on a personal and professional level and in a world where the economy, occupying a growing space in man's *raison d'être*, is increasingly uncertain, complex, rushed, or urgent.

One reason for which the economy, here understood as the governing element of man's being, implies not only complexity but also a sense of urgency is that one such understanding is far from being universally accepted by all: without addressing in detail the complexities of Islamic extremism, it is clear that the attacks of September 11, 2001 testify to the refusal of certain peoples to accept the aforementioned reality. Be it motivated by a desire to impose their own means of gaining power and influence, or by the desire sought out by some for a truly pious world, the violence and extremism that lead to the September 11 attacks demonstrate and symbolize an undeniable form of resistance to the political influence, symbol of the economic weight, of the American state. Hypothesizing that contemporary, economic power serves the interests and desires of some at the expense of the greater good springs from resistance to the universal nature of economic power. Those seeking to counterbalance or even eliminate the growing influence of economics from man's existence adhere to the aforementioned reasoning: desiring to do so acknowledges the existence of its antithesis, that the economy constitutes the fundamental governance of man's existence. Establishing this relationship between man and economy is probably not the result of a conscious or voluntary effort. It would be more accurate to assert that the economy, rather than politics or philosophy, is the dominant, contemporary means for expressing man's desire for power. In other words, alongside fear reigns desire, especially the desire for power. And if at all man is conscious of his own fear for survival, it is a result of the desire of those who seek power, who are able to leverage the means for acquiring such power, and who succeed in imposing the resulting requisites for existence on everyone else. Since economy is the dominant means in contemporary power struggles, economic life is the real-life symbol of a world that accomplishes, creates, constrains, and alienates man. It is also a power that is currently being challenged by other voices.

Understanding how and why the economy is at the center of our conception of time, regardless of our individual opinions with regard to time in that role, implies conceiving and understanding fully the construct of time in today's world. But before doing so we must fathom why it is that finding one's place in the contemporary economy, or perhaps even struggling against it, is requisite to survival.

2
Insurrection

Abstract: *Renaissance humanism made clear the notion of control. Writers like Machiavelli, Descartes and Hobbes aimed at this very objective: making humans able to get rid of "nature"—be it human or non-human. Getting rid of "nature" would become possible through the development of a new scientific method. Despite the 21st century changes, our sciences and consequent techniques and technologies result from the Renaissance scientific revolution. Our lives are exceptionally under the sway of economics because modern economic life is rooted in the scientific way of understanding reality, the political one included—which is necessarily a way to transform and to appropriate it.*

Keywords: *control; Descartes; Hobbes; humanism; Machiavelli; modern sciences; technologies*

Bibard, Laurent. *Sexuality and Globalization: An Introduction to a Phenomenology of Sexualities.*
New York: Palgrave Macmillan, 2014.
DOI: 10.1057/9781137469298.0007.

It is useful to understand the Ancient Greek origins of the term "economy" without narrowing its meaning: that which "governs the home" and encompasses the intimate and family sphere. Where its most immediate needs are concerned, this sphere consists of satisfying man's vital requirements—food, clothing, and shelter—which, when fulfilled, allow him to procreate. It can therefore be argued that satisfying man's vital needs is fundamental, at least in part, to the economy's serving as a paradigm, a daily reality and a symbol of power. Notwithstanding the creation, development, unbalancing, and propelling of the satisfaction of these vital needs by desire and imagination, satisfaction of desire remains the underlying dynamic. The economy plays a preeminent role in man's ability to live and survive thereby promoting a fear of failure that consequently drives his preoccupation with meeting both his vital and trivial needs. And yet man's fear of failure also cultivates within him an archaic desire to succeed as well as to master those processes he undertakes in order to satisfy his desires and needs. Sooner or later, on both an individual and a community level, man is at least in part motivated by the need to master that which he undertakes since it will either directly or indirectly impact his desire for living as opposed to his fear of dying. As far as our lives are concerned, lives of which we are sometimes the recalcitrant incubators, this motive is the link that binds, energizes, and paralyzes us. The economy's reign as the focal point of man's modern-day activities is dictated by his desire to live, his want to control the outcomes of his enterprises, as opposed to his fear of death: his absolute and unquestionable lack of control. How is it, in the early 21st century, that man basically focuses the entirety of his actions around the economy, around his desire to live and his fear of death, each of which diminishes the meaning of his life to but one amongst many others?

This question is only relevant so long as man believes that he has goals, activities, or sources of meaning for his existence other than his own life. Various forms of suicide: individual, collective, warlike, orderly, or anarchical, organized by commanders, consciously and voluntarily deliberate, highlight the morose side of this posit which can also be constructively evidenced, at least in part, by all forms of activity and of independent sources that give meaning to the economic aspect of human life much like writing is an attempt at understanding and awareness.

Although the effort to understand how and why the economy dominates our perception of time is neither entirely economic nor technoscientific; it does depend, at least partially, on current economic and scientific trends. Such an effort must be inspired from a place outside of the realm of the contemporary economy and the scientific and human techniques that support it. Working under the assumption that modern technology and sciences nourish an economy that in turn vectors them, the attempt to identify how our time is organized is neither "scientific" nor technical in the contemporary sense of the word. By this same logic, neither the human nor the natural sciences is an effective cipher in our perception of time. The aspiration to comprehend our time cannot, in fact, rely on history as a science capable of demystifying the genesis of the economic prerogative over other human activity. As is the case for all social studies, our understanding of history as a modern, social study depends mostly on a distant regard that we are attempting here. Nor can the preferred method for doing so repose on methodologies and epistemological work that have proven effective in analyzing social science, natural science, or social studies. We will thus be able to gain any methodological insight only at the conclusion of our current essay: a successful analysis alone will give way to a methodological construct allowing for and validating the process. The extent to which the following assumptions are deemed authoritative will be the barometer of our success.

The first of these assumptions concerns man's contemporary preoccupation with wanting to live and his correlated fear of death, both of which compel him to seek an even greater mastery, and therefore control, over the outcomes of his actions in the context of an uncertain and complex world. It is also plausible that man's aforementioned desire to live, though a universal one, can be traced back, in time and in space, to what is commonly known as the European Renaissance. Our objective is not in the least an exhaustive historical account in the modern sense of the word. Rather our primary focus will be to pinpoint the origin of a process that has overtaken us with or without our consent. To this end we will allude to two seminal texts that exemplify, though not singularly so, the event by which man turned his attention inward. The first of these texts is an excerpt of Descartes' *Discourse on the Method* first published in 1637. The second excerpt is from Machiavelli's *Prince* (dating from 1513).[1] The first of these excerpts is as follows:

> But as soon as I had acquired some general notions respecting physics, and beginning to make trial of them in various particular difficulties, had observed how far they can carry us, and how much they differ from the principles that have been employed up to the present time, I believed that I

could not keep them concealed without sinning grievously against the law by which we are bound to promote, as far as in us lies, the general good of mankind. For by them I perceived it to be possible to arrive at knowledge highly useful in life; and in room of the speculative philosophy usually taught in the schools, to discover a practical, by means of which, knowing the force and action of fire, water, air, the stars, the heavens, and all the other bodies that surround us, as distinctly as we know the various crafts of our artisans, we might also apply them in the same way to all the uses to which they are adapted, and thus render ourselves the lords and possessors of nature. And this is a result to be desired, not only in order to the invention of an infinity of arts, by which we might be enabled to enjoy without any trouble the fruits of the earth, and all its comforts, but also and especially for the preservation of health, which is without doubt, of all the blessings of this life, the first and fundamental one; for the mind is so intimately dependent upon the condition and relation of the organs of the body, that if any means can ever be found to render men wiser and more ingenious than hitherto, I believe that it is in medicine they must be sought for.[2]

In this familiar passage from *Discourse on the Method,* Descartes explicitly states his decision to reveal what he had learned during his studies of physics insofar as it diverged significantly from those principles (of knowledge) "that have been employed up to the present time." Just as Machiavelli had done a century earlier, Descartes challenges, in that which amongst other things is relegated to the past, the way in which man conceives knowledge. The new relationship to knowledge seeks to obey the "the law by which we are bound to promote, as far as in us lies, the general good of mankind," a law of unknown origin, if not from man himself, for he who enunciates and obliges it. The "general good of mankind" can be attained through new knowledge, or a new way of engaging knowledge that is "highly useful in life." Contrary to the speculative philosophy that had dominated thinking to that point, this practical knowledge is ultimately manifest in the work of artisans. Today the ultimate model of knowledge is the economy: building on the "various crafts of our artisans," we can now construct factories, and conceive new industries such as agribusiness and the service industry. Descartes, just like Bacon, his predecessors, as well as those who followed, belongs to the group of philosophers who orient the use of knowledge to the benefit of man's existence in the here and now, one that is above all economic in nature. When he adds that this new approach to knowledge "...is to be desired not only in order to the invention of an infinity of arts by which we might be enabled to enjoy without any trouble the fruits of the earth, and all its comfort," but "also and especially for the preservation of health" (Descartes), he suggests that the mind's well-being is dependent on the health of the body and that the latter must be looked after because its health ensures that of the mind thereby rendering man "wiser and more ingenious." Making men wiser and more ingenious is tantamount to making them "lords and possessors of nature," the central premise of the text in question. An underlying tension galvanizes Descartes' thinking: on the one hand, he recognizes that health is a precondition to the positive conditioning of the body since an unhealthy body renders useless the mind with which man thinks. In short, man's life counts more than all else. But his life will lack meaning so long as it is left to its own devices: life takes on meaning when used as springboard for the continuous improvement of the conditions into which man is born.³ In sum, human life takes on meaning and value proportional to the development of man's acquisition of useful knowledge from his world, learned by imitating (its) artisans—even if he does so with the tacit goal of becoming an ever wiser and more able master of nature.

First account: Descartes, who for this was acknowledged by Hegel as a "hero of modern thought," makes his contribution in a resolute and decisive manner that coincides with a turning point of thought toward the benefit of practical life. The incessant improvements to everyday life brought about by the continuous strides made in science and technology that were based first on industrial and ultimately on economic models was expected to procure the general good for all. Let's examine our second excerpt.

> I conclude, thus, that when fortune varies and men remain obstinate in their modes, men are happy while they are in accord, and as they come into discord, unhappy. I judge this indeed, that it is better to be impetuous than cautious, because fortune is a woman; and it is necessary, if one wants to hold her down, to beat her and strike her down. And one sees that she lets herself be won more by the impetuous than by those who proceed coldly. And so always, like a woman, she is the friend of the young, because they are less cautious, more ferocious, and command her with more audacity.⁴

The fundamental importance of Machiavelli's ideas, as they appear at the end of chapter XXV of *The Prince*, should not be overlooked. One can only wonder what an author henceforth known in most circles, including the most profane, sought to communicate, beyond a male-chauvinistic or even misogynistic discourse, by the commonly used expression "Machiavellianism." That he has become such a common, household name testifies to his level of skillfulness with the pen. It is useful to recognize this characterization even if it means distancing ourselves from the world that he helps create.

While "fortune is a woman" and "varies," men remain "obstinate in their modes." The misfortune of the latter is interwoven with the changes in the former from the moment their paths diverge. Changes in fortune or "chance," in the uncontrollable reaches of life, are a source of misfortune for those who are incapable of adapting to fortune. Though Machiavelli's solution is simple, that men must master fortune through the use of force, it presupposes that the use of said force will suit fortune. Man is capable of shaping the world to his liking provided that he possess both the capability and especially the desire. Doing so he will soon realize that fortune awaits his decision and that it prefers the audacious brazenness and the irreverent ferociousness of he who will confront and subdue her with cold prudence, of he who lies in wait for the mercy of fortune's shifting nature. Using a more elegant and sober tone, Descartes imagines men "as lords and possessors of nature," more in terms of knowledge than of action, and thus joins Machiavelli in his vision. In other words, though the two men differ in premise and in style, a natural result of differing states of mind, Descartes and Machiavelli express the same desires for and assumptions about man: his general well-being, or his ability to sidestep misfortune, is attained by controlling and possessing nature or by the submission of fortune—or alternatively by subduing "reality" to man's desires. Machiavelli's metaphorical use of the feminine as fortune's twin polishes the analogy of the authors' respective stances.

Descartes' implicitly advances an argument identical to that of Machiavelli in which the latter asserts that fortune, because it is woman, takes pleasure in submitting to man and conforming to the audacious, irreverent, and rash ferociousness of youth's desires. Woman, as the fertile ground of reproduction, is the symbol and originator of the very mystery of all speech that begins with man's anonymous existence. As such woman is the archetypal symbol of "fortune," or that which is, in the world into which man is born, unverifiable, uncontrollable and that upon which he is fundamentally dependent. A woman's round, fertilized stomach is the other face of what man sometimes calls "God."[5] This is why Machiavelli makes the decision to accept and advocate fortune as a controllable phenomenon. The very mystery of human life may itself be forced into submission by those to whom it gives life. Anonymous at birth these lives, with time and maturity, acquire a name and language. They start with a cry at birth and soon gain an identity as responsible, free, and individual beings. Though the desire to control life and birth was not a novel one, man's conviction that it were *possible* to control one or the other was radically so. This idea is not the result of a single philosopher's spontaneous, political decision but rather the effect of a series of decisions made in the same spirit as Descartes'. When, according to the logic of his decision to envision man as "master and possessor of nature," Descartes elevates medicine to the role of the science most capable of improving man's skillfulness he, just as Machiavelli, makes the process of life that will soon be capable of speech, of thought and of decision, and even of procreation, the object of his work. Through the process of gestation the feminine is the ultimate manifestation and symbol of the creation of human life. Independent of Machiavelli's personal experiences and far from the male chauvinism and the misogyny to which we earlier alluded, Descartes and his Florentine counterpart share the same hope: that by shedding light on the mysteries of the world, man might be able to control them thereby facilitating his ultimate quest to improve his life on Earth. Recalling the true meaning of the Heraclitean adage "nature likes to hide," it becomes clear that one of the most important outcomes of man's desire to master and control "fortune" or "nature" lies in the opening of the body be it by way of weapons, surgical procedures or by dissection.

* * *

The two author's ideas reconverge beyond their shared view of the mastery of nature and of fortune. They also agree on the objective of doing so: Machiavelli, perhaps more so than Descartes, sets his sights on that which is useful, that which extols an efficient realism. This is how he opens his heart to his readers in the beginning of chapter XV of *The Prince*:

> But, it being my intention to write a thing which shall be useful to him who apprehends it, it appears to me more appropriate to follow up the real truth of the matter than the imagination of it; for many have pictured republics and principalities which in fact have never been known or seen, because how one lives is so far distant from how one ought to live, that he who neglects what is done for what ought to be done, sooner effects his ruin than his preservation...[6]

Like Descartes, Machiavelli finds it useless to daydream about impractical worlds, rather he favors the sharing of knowledge, opinions, valuable or "profitable" ruminations, especially where these are effective in extending man's life on Earth by way of either his political authority or his biological health. The idea of political authority will later become a central theme for Thomas Hobbes who, inspired by the work of his predecessors, will introduce the contemporary, political idea of State sovereignty. Hobbes' fundamental opposition to his predecessors, especially Aristotle and Plato whom he relegates to the past for they are, for him, passé, lies in his belief in the origins of man's collective existence. Contrary to Aristotle, whose philosophical approach to the question of man had dominated European thought for more than 2000 years, Hobbes theorizes that life's political or collective nature is far from being inherent to human life. Here is what he says of a life left to its own devices:

> And because the condition of man...is a condition of war of every one against every one, in which case every one is governed by his own reason, and there is nothing he can make use of that may not be a help unto him in preserving his life against his enemies; it followeth that in such a condition every man has a right to every thing, even to another's body. And therefore, as long as this natural right of every man to every thing endure, there can be no security to any man, how strong or wise so ever he be, of living out the time which nature ordinarily allow men to live.[7]

According to Hobbes the natural or native state into which all humans are born is a state of war pitting man against man (the infamous *homo homini lupus*) in a struggle for the scarce resources rationally sought out by each and every human for survival. Scarcity can be defined as the result of multiple individuals, equal in rights, seeking out the same object or resource capable of satisfying given desires or vital needs. Following this logic, Hobbes' reasoning can be summarized as the following: each and every human, "governed by his own reason," realizes that, in the absence of an outside authority responsible for delegating the attribution of resources necessary to every individual's survival, life is a constant struggle whose only meaning is to preserve one's existence provided that life itself does not end during the struggles meant to preserve it. In the absence of that which "he can make use of that may not be a help unto him in preserving his life against his enemies" life is an absurd, yet a simple story "full of sound and fury." Therein lies the solution to this problem: man must find time for a peaceful existence, a time during which he lets down his guard, so that he may find meaning for his life, and so that he does not perish while defending his place amongst other men. Creating such a peaceful existence is only possible when a single, third party is granted the authority to enforce laws upon all citizens: such is the modern notion of the sovereign State. *Homo homini deus*.

Seeking to institute and justify politics as a newfound object of science, this modern notion of life is, by construction, governed according to an *economic* principle: the science of allocating, distributing and even creating resources that are, by nature, rare. This principle takes for granted that men are free, equal, and rational—or, above all calculating in terms of their vital needs, desires and fears.

* * *

The human aim of serving man in the here and now, in the routine of and to the benefit of his biological life, finds its roots in Machiavelli and was propagated by thinkers such as Descartes and Hobbes. Such an existence is seemingly driven from within by the powerful momentum that motivates man to control his actions with the ultimate goal of living. Man's desire to control his actions presupposes an intent to understand and control "nature" or "fortune," be it by force, as well as the existence of a humanity composed of free, equal, rational beings that are in a constant state of war with one another as they seek out rare resources. These resources are necessary for survival and if possible should allow for a good, if not happy existence. Finally, it must be noted that the change in man's role and place on Earth implied a shift in perspective. Descartes was forthcoming in his belief that knowledge "for the sake of knowledge" was losing ground to knowledge at the service of everyday life. Leo Strauss will echo the importance of a notion also held by Machiavelli as early as *The Prince*, in the second part of chapter XVIII: "men in general judge more by their eyes than by their hands; for everyone can see but few can feel."

According to Machiavelli a man's hands are his extensions for experiencing the world tactilely and thus are his most important tools of observation. If Machiavelli's philosophy proves true, then as Marx reiterates in *The German Ideology*: knowing amounts to transforming. In a world in which learning is an efficient endeavor in the creation and control that man employs in order to extract a comfortable life, knowing "for the sake of wisdom," a now obsolete idea that renders insignificant what Descartes will call learning that is "valuable for life," loses its standing as a noble cause. Let's not forget that, Hobbes, too, supposes and extols the putting into perspective of knowledge given that the natural state of man, as Hobbes himself says, is a theoretical artifice destined to assure efficient self-defense and the ultimate sovereignty of the political process. An expected result of political control at all cost would be a conception of natural rights that is anything but natural, but that is instead justified by the ends that one such notion is meant to serve. Man's perception of his world is such that he will henceforth perceive his desire to transform this world, in which he is an active element, as either a natural or divine right, a perception that will carry over into the domains of good and evil, of the just and unjust as much as it does in questions of that which is true or untrue. In other words man is only inspired to fulfill his own desires.

* * *

It is not our aim to identify causal series that would have brought about a transformation in European "culture" from one state or "paradigm" to another. It is, however, clear that during and after the parade of Renaissance authors who affirmed, proclaimed and defended the concept hereto elicited with regard to man's place, role and right in the world, a qualitative change took place regarding that which is understood to be evident and valuable in life. This change is especially visible through the incontestable inroads made by economics not just in the realm of politics but also in the entirety of mankind's existence.

Our principle objective hereto has been to elucidate those ideas that will guide our analysis toward a few pointed issues so that we may conceptualize the world into which we were born. Without naming them explicitly we have alluded to several, broad assumptions that have indirectly made way for the economy to resonate throughout all human activity. These lines of thought are grounded in a conception of human beings:

1. who are not initially calculating or "rational"
2. whose lives are initially connected, not individuated, by relationships whose nature remains to be understood
3. who are perhaps moved by more than the desire to lead comfortable lives and the fear of dying a potentially violent death, but also by the wish to learn for the sake of learning
4. who neither assume that they can nor wish to control "nature" or "fortune" by becoming an enlightened person, but who admit to the usefulness of mystery in the world, or the insurmountable nature of obscurity on Earth and perhaps elsewhere

The aforementioned shift in paradigm occurred around the Renaissance era, and largely as a result of it. This renaissance can be described as an act of defiance with regard to the political and intellectual power, largely

Christian in nature, which reigned in Europe at the time. With this information in mind it is natural to wonder, so as to understand better the anthropology implicitly rejected by Machiavelli, Descartes, Hobbes, and their contemporaries, to what extent the affirmation of a modern, or "economistic," anthropology of man is Christian in origin.

Our investigation is less than ever a "historical" one, in the modern sense of the term—particularly from a positivist approach. Rather, and as it has been duly defended, our proposal is shaped by an interpretation of the secular future of Christianity that will largely result from a critical approach to the current understanding of history—not just Western but world history. What we are suggesting with regard to the processes of Christian theology is thus strictly based on the actions of those who, starting in 16th century Europe, attempted to distance themselves from it. It is not so much Christian dogma that interests us, but rather the reaction of the European humanists and their emulators to this dogma that will be the focal point of our investigation.

Notes

1. Cf Strauss L., *Thoughts on Machiavelli* (University of Washington Press, 1958), and "The Three Waves of Modernity "*Political Philosophy, Six Essays by Leo Strauss*, (Indianapolis and New York, 1975).
2. Descartes, Rene. *Discourse on the Method of Rightly Conducting the Reason and Seeking Truth in the Sciences*. (1st World Library-Literary Society: UK, 2005).
3. Cf John Locke's "Of Property", *Of Civil Government*, chapter V.
4. Machiavelli, Niccolò. *The Prince*, end of chapter XXV, Trans. Harvey C. Mansfield. (Chicago : The University of Chicago Press, 1998).
5. *Genesis* 4,1.
6. Machiavelli, Niccolò. *The Prince*, chapter XV, beginning.
7. Hobbes, Thomas. *Leviathan*, beginning of chapter XIV, "Of first and second natural laws, and of contracts." (Penguin Books, 1968).

3
Christianity, Paganism, Judaism: The Fury of Practice

Abstract: *This chapter traces the Renaissance revolution back to the interlacing of the two roots Christianity's roots: the Jewish and the pagan. Judaism and paganism oppose each other on the basis of monotheism and polytheism. This frontal opposition may be understood as an opposition between ultimately theoretical and practical approaches of life. The Christian theology of perfection mixes theoretical and practical approaches to life, or contemplation-oriented and action-oriented attitudes. This theology sooner or later makes room for humans claiming to control their lives and world by controlling nature.*

Keywords: *Christianity; Judaism; paganism; practice; subsumption; theory*

Bibard, Laurent. *Sexuality and Globalization: An Introduction to a Phenomenology of Sexualities.* New York: Palgrave Macmillan, 2014.
DOI: 10.1057/9781137469298.0008.

The philosophers hitherto mentioned wielded their pens at a time, in Europe, when the "true" foundations of knowledge and action were thought to have been lost. These foundations were allegedly obscured from view by Christianity that, while synonymous with a political and intellectual authority, was inconsistent in separating the Church from politics. The repeated attempts to resuscitate thought, this time with a novel grasp on action, opposed a still-dominant Christian theology that was often the driving force of the new thinkers who opposed it. The pagan and Jewish roots of Christianity were in turn a source of direction and nourishment of its own affirmation. At the heart of the Christianity that had been transformed into a reigning political and intellectual power, labors "real" Christianity whose spirit has been guarded for future rediscovery by its "Book"; within "real" Christianity continually Christianity is continually galvanized by the values that define it. Judaism is irrefutably part of these values.

Judaism

Judaism is built upon the rejection of that which it does not want to be. The monotheistic assertion that typifies it is formulated both collectively and negatively: we are not linked with those who believe in multiple gods and therefore in none. Adherence to a polytheistic system will ultimately reduce the gods to behaving in an overly-human manner since they would be prone to unavoidable power struggles amongst themselves. Divine power can be vested in only one. Alternatively, the absolute character of an all-powerful god renders him inaccessible to humans both in terms of understanding him and potentially appropriating him. In such a system the deadly sin of pride is not only the most serious that man can commit, the one that he commits when tasting the forbidden fruit, but also the most absurd: man's struggle against "God" as it is described in the Jewish tradition is, by construction, futile. However since God is almighty, and thus creates his image and imposes his will by rituals that are themselves impenetrable, humans, too, are incapable of ascertaining the legitimacy of a divine revelation through their innate senses of observation. They can only believe what is revealed to them or is imposed upon them as a model of a respectable life and are therefore reticent with regard to the word of the prophets. The Jewish canon in its entirety is marked by the incessant and painful effort to distinguish right from wrong. Being Jewish is, in essence, choosing to believe by continually forcing oneself to discriminate between right and wrong and therefore between the just and the unjust. Being Jewish means a continuous effort to conform to the spirit of a Book that is understood to be incomplete. Being Jewish is a persistent attempt to maintain faith despite an insurmountable and abyssal uncertainty as to the veracity of the underlying belief system. Being Jewish can be defined as the ability to err and fail, with or without understanding why. It means being prone to doing harm, without realizing it, despite having good intentions. One of Judaism's defining structures is an expectation that constantly overwhelms the effort of those who wish to conform to its commandments for there is a constant tension between the effort to do and the inherent doubt with regard to the possible outcome of thought and action. Beginning with Moses' revelation of the commandments, Judaism has been organized as a community ordered by a succession of rules that dictate how to interpret the sacred texts: Judaism is ultimately an act of responsibility. Individual responsibility is henceforth understood as an individual's responsibility to the community of people who endeavor to respect the law, the commandments, the impenetrable import of divine will that can become the obligation of a people before the god that they have chosen.

Man's decision to believe or disbelieve, to conform or to waver, is a political one since any of these paths places one in accordance with the beliefs of some and in conflict with that of others who themselves are categorized as either believers or non-believers. Judaism is one of the most exacting examples of the painful negotiation between truth and action: the prophets who speak in absolute truth are at the same time sources of fear and dissonance, for those too-human individuals who were not chosen to hear the humanly inaccessible voice of God. According to Judaism, anything and everything can, at any moment, be deformed, transformed or destroyed as a result of impenetrable decisions. Value is absent from everything because nothing can stand up in the face of the all-powerful divine whose first accomplishment was his own, limitless sovereignty. God is the creator of the sky and the Earth, of the birds, of the sea's fish, of plants and of animals, and God is the creator of both man and woman. He obeys his own will, when he wishes and how he wishes. The existence of a "nature," any nature, that can resist divine will and action is counterintuitive to Orthodox Judaism[1]: man's sole duty is to live according to the law and the words of the prophets—man must make do with the elusive character of God's word. Indeed, man must make do in light of the struggle between conforming to God's law by believing, and disobeying by doubting, a struggle which is aggravated by a uniquely and fundamentally human characteristic that is undoubtedly the fruit of divine will: it is in the image of God that man and woman were created.[2] Man is but the infinitely humble reflection of the *image* of God; but the image *of God* suggests that deep within man is the possibility of divinity, a relative all-powerfulness over the creatures and self, the faculty to unite with himself as well as a gift of creation. Thus man may be tempted to see himself as God and, by doing so, become a sinner. He is therefore placed in a situation of irrefutable and infinitely painful liberty, infinitely responsible for his choices and for his faith. Both doubt and temptation are requisite to faith, an idea reaffirmed by the monotheisms to follow, each in its own way.

For the Jew, judgment is reserved for his acts: knowing only has meaning in its biblical connotation which itself is defined as respecting the divine word that commands humans to "be fruitful and multiply."

Paganism

At its advent, Christianity was the fusion of the Jewish world with the "others." For Christianity, these other worlds were "pagan." At the time of Jesus Christ, Jews imagined the pagan world, though not exclusively so, as being synonymous with the Roman Empire whose own roots were directly inspired by Greek Paganism, the birthplace of philosophy. Understanding Christianity is tantamount to describing the way in which it resembles and differentiates itself from paganism. For the purposes of this essay, paganism is characterized by the emphasis that it places on the concept of "nature," notably present in the Greek mythology, and then widely adopted by the Romans, that implies nature's ultimate triumph over the Greek gods. In seemingly risqué fashion, the god's weakness is especially evident through Zeus' sexual desire. The idea of "nature" in Greek is referred to as *physis*, a term that suggests "growth": nature is that which grows or which makes things happen, grow, mature, fade away, and become corrupt. In the Immortals' minds, nature's cycle of being: birth, growth, maturation, decline, and corruption is more powerful than they or even their own eternity. In one way or another, nature and the pagan notion of divinity are interrelated thereby placing paganism at the antipodes of the monotheistic, Jewish tradition. The Jewish rejection of paganism is central to defining Judaism. It is important to recall that Jewish theology and Greek philosophy, respectively rooted in the polysemous notions of "god" and of "nature," developed independently of one another. Only after independently forming relatively coherent and complete systems, at least in their own estimation, did they meet some three centuries before the advent of Christianity: this new form of religion, *the* new religion, that attempted to impose itself, and, in the eyes of some, succeeded in doing so.

The pagan approach to nature, which we will call "Greek" paganism, is shaped and symbolized by the dawn of philosophy. The original term is taken from *philo-sophia*, "the love of wisdom." Greek wisdom was implicitly determined by nature's hegemony over the Greek gods. Even they were less powerful than nature, symbolized in mythology by the sexual desire of the god of all gods who descended from Kronos, thus *a fortiori* men. The most prominent commandment, in the Greek tradition, that parallels one such conception of the world is that man, so as to ensure his own happiness, must live in harmony with the world into which he is born. Doing so implies understanding, or knowing, its proportions. Knowledge is above all the means by which man can be in phase with nature—in both the sense of appropriateness of things and their conformity to the idea that man must be in equilibrium with the world—and therefore be happy. Knowledge, in the Greek or pagan meaning of the word, can only be understood as a means of respecting the exactness of objects and therefore does not depend on the arbitrary nature of man's will but rather on the natural cycle of birth and death of which man is unavoidably a part. The best way to live, according to the Greeks, is to understand nature to the best of one's ability and to concede what man can learn from such knowledge. The natural cycle of birth and death, not always evident, but irrefutably eternal, lends to at least a partial understanding of some part of man who himself is born from this very cycle. The humanity in question is an integral part of a sequence from which it cannot, by definition, extract itself. Doing so would imply violating nature's laws. This same humanity is ultimately aware of good and evil as well as of the just and unjust because it differentiates between right and wrong. This humanity is in clear opposition to the humanity conceived by the Orthodox Jews for whom right and wrong are a result of good and evil or of just and unjust.

Christianity—Crucifixion

At the moment when, independently of historical events, Christianity brings Judaism and paganism into the same theoretical space, it forcibly unites two diametrically opposed theologies. It is a round peg in a square hole or the cross one must bear.

Nothing is more "natural" indeed than the Christian claim that Jesus Christ is the son of his father. It is for this very reason, this "natural" relationship, that Orthodox Judaism must reject such a hypothesis, since "God" is infinitely above and set apart from anything that could be construed as "natural." It runs contrary to the very foundation of Jewish theology that the man who claims to be the Messiah also claims to be the son of his father. This particular breach of the law is called "incarnation." The most significant and therefore most meaningful end result of divine incarnation is the death of God: for the Jewish God, incarnation means being subjected to the very first of nature's laws, the cycle of life and death—in other words the death of all mortal beings. If Jesus Christ came to take away the sins of the world, he did so by suffering as all humans do from the consequences of the original sin: living with the knowledge that one will eventually die. The death of God is the logical end result of his incarnation.

It is clear that divine incarnation alone, without a sequel, would result in God's bending to the pagan power of nature. If He transcends nature, however, the end result will be very different. Transcending nature is tantamount to foiling death and inexorably perpetuating existence. Transcending death amounts to challenging death's unalterable reality, revealing the all-powerful nature of its contrary, the all-powerful divine. The resurrection of Jesus Christ essentially carries out His decision of incarnation and therefore of death. Foretelling Jesus' resurrection from the dead, and that after three days his tomb would be empty, is both fundamental and unique to the dogma of Christianity. In other words, believing in the resurrection of Christ is the foundation for all Orthodox Christian belief.[3]

Christianity developed as a result of its own periods of unrest, divergence, catastrophes, and transformations that were both spontaneous and incited. It witnessed the advent of the monastic movement, orthodox schisms, and much later, during the era that interests us the most, the protestant and Catholic schisms. It was furthermore witness to its own Gnostic heresies, mystics and finally the inevitable, theological controversies brought on by its eminently illogical affirmation, especially where the mother of Christ is concerned: she who is "nature" in every sense of the word yet, at the same time of a divine, or at least sacred order albeit ambiguously so. It is not the history of Christianity that interests us in our current investigation, but rather how the aforementioned men of the Renaissance manipulated it. Their perspective, of particular interest in this essay, can be summarized as follows.

The subsumption of nature to divine power that defines the Christian dogma profoundly alters the essence of the rapport that converted Jews have with divinity as well as that of the pagans with nature. In light of these supposed transformations, for both Jews and pagans, maintaining their respective relationships to the divine and to nature will be a delicate and fragile, if not debatable effort. For various reasons, the reversal would be even more difficult for the pagans than for the Jews. The subsumption of pagan "nature" in the direction of an all-powerful holiness will sooner or later give rise to a Judeo-Christian anthropology—first *Judeo*-Christian and then Judeo-*Christian*. For the *Judeo*-Christian approach, the primary sentiments are those of allegiance, doubt and fear that characterize the Jewish approach to their God on the one hand, to action (sooner or later creative action) according to the law on the other, and finally to man's potential to pride himself to the point of being on equal plane, as a creator, with God. The Judeo-*Christian* approach implies that Jewish anthropology exists uniquely according the logic of a prerequisite recognition of pagan anthropology that can be characterized as violent, given the implicit duplicity. Pagan anthropology emphasizes man's essential place in nature that he is incapable of transcending alone—lest he believe, or, in other words, convert. It is important to remember that by occupying this "essential place" man will have no higher a calling to which to devote himself than conforming to the "nature" in which he takes part and of which he is just one part. Conforming to nature eventually implies knowing it, a fragmentary attempt that is carried out, in Aristotle's words, by total, active reception through contemplation[4]: contrary to the Jewish man who is above all a creator, the pagan, or Greek man is ultimately contemplative and thoughtful.[5] Jewish anthropology, transformed by Christianity, by recognizing the utility of understanding and knowing "nature" on its own terms in order to raise it to new heights, to over-nature it, to perfect it or to elevate it to the level of the divine. Christianity's recognition of the "theoretical," pagan approach[6] is evident in its transformation into an ultimately *useful* tool for the creative endeavors of the Judeo-Christian man. Admitting that humanity itself is an act that over-natures or perfects nature implies an initial recognition of nature and admitting that the creative will of man, an image of the creative will of God, propels this infinitely powerful over-naturing or perfection and implies forcing into submission the natural, contemplative approach to the negative and creative approach that is above-all *practical*. Imposing man's creative attitude on his theoretical (Greek) existence transforms his life into a modern, applied, scientific approach that is by definition oriented and propelled by its potential *utility* in this world. The birth of modern science, claimed to be of Christian origin,[7] boils down to the eminently practical transformation of the contemplative Greek, or pagan, attitude that henceforth defines all science as an elaboration of *theories* of objects that are sooner or later empirically verified. In other words *objects* are gauged according to their utility and practicality. The secularization of Christianity to which Descartes and his contemporaries endeavored implies that knowledge for "the sake of knowledge" is, in principle, relegated to the past.

By renouncing the culture and political heritage imposed by an intellectually dominant Christianity, the Renaissance philosophers essentially appropriated this heritage anew despite their attempt to deny its importance. And yet part of this heritage is the word of Jesus Christ, commanding man, amongst other actions, to do as He did: choosing to believe in Him implies repeating His resurrection. This repetition must be carried out not only symbolically or through prayer, but rather through practice or for the "greater good of all men" the meaning of which is paramount to giving man's creative skill a considerable advantage over his contemplative capacities. It also means according limitless power to man's will to the detriment of "understanding"[8] or intelligence. The secularization of Christianity has resulted in a liberation of man's will, thereby leaving him free in his sinful desire to be God's equal through his own, Earthly endeavors. Henceforth it is his desire that commands, independent of any law, especially those of Judaism and nature. Far from symbolizing man's constraints or limits, scientific "law" represents the logical base upon which man's will is formed through action. Man considers his will as absolute, supreme, prevailing, an arbiter, impenetrable, unpredictable, and all-powerful. Finally, His will, in the image of the glorious and embodied God, is always that of an individual born free, rational and equal who, as such, is born reasonable, or worse, already reasoned. Man is henceforth calculating to the extent that this state leads him to a comfortable existence in his world. He alternatively fears and yearns for such an existence without unwarranted interest for knowledge or the beauty of his world. He assumes, in the end, and wishes in fact, for his control of the world to be absolute. His image of absolute control is ultimately analogous to the way in which nature is paralyzed by the glory of the resurrection of Christ.

* * *

Hereto we have observed worlds in which humans are perceived as being a priori no more rational than reasonable; in which they are motivated by neither the sole desire to live comfortably, if possible, in this world (or particularly, for one of the worlds in question, in conformity) nor the fear of dying. Likewise they assume it neither possible nor desirable to control the world into which they are born if only because doing so would mean recognizing this world's nature or its god. The present era, inaugurated by the likes of Machiavelli, Descartes, Hobbes, and their successors deliberately refutes those of the Jewish and pagan worlds hereto described that serve as the dual pillars of Christianity. This very world is likewise a rejection of the Christian world when it is not secularized.

Let us thus take a moment to review what has been said thus far.

We began with an observation of the economy's resonance in today's world by highlighting a few of its negative manifestations. We then accounted for the Christian origins not just of modern science but also of the omnipresent economy by demonstrating the characteristics that are unique to Christianity and that allowed the Humanists to affirm, during the European Renaissance, man's supreme power within these worlds. To that end, we characterized Christianity's dual pillars: Judaism and paganism (Roman and Greek, amongst others). Contemporary economism's success lies partly in the effacement of these worlds in which mystery existed in the form of the resurrection of a god who died as an equal to the most humble of men; in which the wisest of men bowed before the ultimate mystery of a nature who hid her creation from man; in which, paradoxically, man forced himself to respect a divine law whose logic was impenetrable. Its defining characteristic is the implicit affirmation that man can know and has an interest in knowing everything about his world in order to ensure his control or mastery of it and for the sake of his survival or even for the comfort of his existence. In this sense, man is defined as a free individual equal to all others, following his changing interests, recoiling from his fears, constantly feeling the need to remain vigilant in a turbulent and chaotic world that is eventually characterized by the inexorable mixing of his fears and desires. The contemporary economic world, which is in many ways synonymous with the contemporary world, is quite consistent with the natural state of man described by Hobbes. Whereas Hobbes introduced this state by affirming and describing it as the artificial, and therefore theoretical and intellectual, root of any *future* political sovereignty, it is quite simply a given in today's practical world. Today's world, according to *Leviathan* is either corrupt or powerless and one in which man lacks the leisure requisite to finding meaning in life. Contemporary man is therefore the very definition of "lacking in time" given his incessant struggle to craft a world that he will then inhabit.

Surprisingly, as harsh as the world may be, it fascinates, interests and mobilizes henceforth, in one way or another, the totality of the human population: the trend whose European origins can be traced back to the 25th century, characterized by economism's spontaneous move to become universal, is now becoming a reality. This can only be comprehended if sufficient weight is given to the importance of the archaic reality of man's desire to control his world, which is achievable only if transparency is assured by an intellectual and practical hold on "nature" that allows man the greatest possible control over the outcomes of his actions. In other words, man's desire to control his world is universal and can be observed as early as the European Renaissance by way of an understanding and institutionalization of this mastery through political action plans, as well as the intellectual approach to knowledge both of which are universally seductive. As Machiavelli points out as early as *The Prince,* it is the Faustian desire to remain young, audacious, commanding, ferocious, and disrespectful toward nature, a nature that, contrary to man's will, spontaneously harbors within itself both the process of aging and death as much as the passing generations and lives.

Contemporary reversals in fortune of the perceived triumph of modern economism and its corollary, the techno-scientific, are however at least partially the reflection of, as well as the source of, measured reservations with regard to its perceived triumph. Man's control over a world in which everyone is expected to calculate his interests freely and rationally, albeit sufficiently manipulated to serve the bottom line of private enterprise, according to pre-determined and wind-swayed possibilities is not a universal value. Considering the path that we have followed hereto, the pre-Christian Jewish and Greek worlds are seemingly the most promising models for seeking out an alternative way to life. When studied comparatively, the Jewish and Greek philosophies of existence correspondingly demonstrate respect for divine commandments and a reflection on nature, or, in other words, one way of expressing the notion of action and another way of expressing the notion of knowledge: they constitute the two, essential ways in which humans can live. It is of utmost importance for the following exercise that we do not engage in a modern historian's work: our goal is not to identify Judaism and Greek paganism as they are or were and as they identify and self-identified at various moments of their existence. The differentiation of these two worlds, of these two models, or of these two ways of living becomes relevant, in terms of this exercise, at the moment that they are brought together by Christianity. This "Christianity" is one we consider in the same way in which we consider the concepts of Judaism and paganism. The belated result of bringing together these two pillars of Christianity is the subsumption of either the knowledge or the contemplative approach to action or to the creative act of man. This subsumption insinuates that practical life is the unique source of meaning in human life, even in theoretical life, and casts doubt on, or at the very least veils the bearings that guide our lives. These bearings are nuanced by their ultimately natural or divine references. If Judaism and Greek paganism both participate in the very stylization that respectively defines them as the origin of action (according to law) and of thought (according to nature), it is clear that each one contributes, to a certain degree and in a rather fertile way, to characterizing all men who are alternately driven to creative or transformative action on the world, or to thinking, knowing or respectfully contemplating it. From this point of view, the world that is today called "the West" is not unique with regard to the other worlds that consist of the past, present and future other than having been the realm where the decision to explicitly affirm, and not solely on the basis of mythology or desire, the ultimate power of man over the world in which he lives. This decision is a result of the definitive subsumption, or at least what is considered to be so, of thought to action, or of knowledge transformed and reduced to the means by which desire serves life. In this perspective, "globalization" cannot exclusively and unilaterally be seen as a universal extension of economic anthropology. To the contrary, it is the meeting point at which contradiction will feed tension for desire and where the hypothetical transparency of the world as well as man's mastery of his world and the implicit affirmation that the transparency and mastery in question are neither desirable nor possible. In "European" terms, the latter can be considered "ancient" or "classic" whereas the former is contemporary or "modern."[9] "Globalization" is therefore the process by which these two schools of thought oppose each other, contradict one another, serve as fertile ground for the other, and highlight differences between opposing desires, attitudes and worlds each in its own turn. Whereas the former positions man as the focal point around which all things occur, the latter supposes that man is grounded in action and thought, two differentiated ways of relating to the world. By illustrating, creating, and justifying the former we sooner or later risk obscuring or losing altogether the aforementioned attitudes, bearings as well as the pre-supposed anthropology of the latter. Understanding time in order to *take* our time requires revealing, to the extent that it is possible, the ties that link and separate man, nature and God, or, in other words, the desire for control, "paganism" and "Judaism" as they have been hereto described. This hypothesis can be sketched out in the following manner.

Before their transformative inclusion into Christianity that has since been secularized by some Humanists, paganism and Judaism symbolize diametrically opposed worlds in Europe that respectively allowed for the predominance of thought and action as a guiding light for the way in which man should live. We can be confident, as was Leo Strauss, in our claim that the respective characteristics of action and thought are distinctive characteristics of human existence: doing is not thinking, and thinking is not doing. The European secularization of Christianity has, however, obliterated this difference by subsuming thought to action: thinking and doing are henceforth identically processed and oriented. The world in which man lives exists in such a way that it blurs the line between the two. "Globalization" consists of the contentious yet ultimate unification of modernity and "ancient." It is the expression of and catalyst for the tension implied by the reversal of the dynamics responsible for shaping the two worlds: the strained contemporaneousness between the Jewish and pagan doctrine is replaced by the fundamental notion of progress resulting from the succession of "ancient" (divided into Jewish and pagan, then Christian and Muslim) and "modern," or in other words, between "non control" and "control." Sketching out one iteration of the notion of globalization implies a vector rotation from a horizontal to a vertical orientation: the former symbolizes the spatially contemporaneousness of the world, the latter is a temporal succession of the two cultures.[10] We obtain the following diagram:

Spatial contemporaneousness of the two worlds

Paganism	Judaism
Nature	"God"
Eternity	Creation
Proportion	Commandments
Contemplation, moderation	Action, obedience
Man as a natural event in nature	Man created in "God's" image

Secular Christianity (semi-transparent mirror)

Chronological succession of cultures

Ancient

Nature alone, Jewish divinity

Modern

Man

Individual who is free, equal and rational

The preceding, heuristic diagram will prove useful in addressing the guiding theme of this essay: the question of time.[11] It will be important to recall that the tension between Judaism and paganism, hereto referred to as Western history, is one that is universal and that can be detected across the history of all civilization and culture. The Judaism and paganism hereto articulated symbolize two, instinctive ways in which all men and societies relate to the world that surrounds them. The desire for and assumption that man can control his world thus takes on a universal character: be it a mythological or "realist" approach, all civilizations and cultures are in part Faustian—the only unique idea afforded by the West is the conviction that man can carry out his worldly desires. In other words, all realities, and therefore all cultures and civilizations contain at the very minimum the three characteristics of humanity: the origin of thought, the origin of action and that of domination as a way by which man affirms himself. All constituent members of the aforementioned realities, cultures and civilizations are therefore concerned. Understood as the tension between dominance and non-dominance (assumed to be one of man's instinctive inclinations) on the one hand and consequently on the other as tension between thought and action, globalization has and will always, in a more or less identifiable and explicit manner, give life to humanity and its preoccupations, contradictions, successes and failures.

There is more. Every individual is, in part, composed of the biological, cultural and social memories that define him. From this point forward it is possible and apposite to affirm that every human is the crossroads of "control" and "non-control," and thus the tension inherent in the crossroads of thought, action, fear and desire. In the same way that being Jewish means, to a certain degree, internalizing paganism, and that being pagan also means feeling part creator and master of his world, so today's man is the incarnation of both "modern" and "ancient." The term "globalization" refers to a series of fundamental, defining tensions that always have been and always will apply on a global, macroscopic or "universal" level as well as on the most microscopic or individual level. This hypothesis merits explanation as it reposes on the following logic.

Judaism and paganism are manifestations of a respectively feminine and masculine sexuality. Their transformation by way of the secularization of Christianity blurs the gender-specific distinction between the two by imposing a "virility" that is both masculine and feminine and thus neither masculine nor feminine. As a result the modern era has been dominated by an asexual virility whose impact on people's lives can only be understood by determining the masculine and feminine characteristics in Man.[12] Doing so is the ultimate objective of this essay. The outcome of such a characterization was evident in the work that followed Edmund Husserl's seminal work in phenomenology. Rather than attempting to understand our daily lives by analyzing their trite outcomes, it is fundamental to this research to understand what constitutes orients and drives the basis of our daily lives. The contemporary dominance of economic virility obscures the way in which each sexuality, masculine and feminine, takes shape. Understanding the way in which each takes shape requires contemplating each in its respective environment. Contemplating each sexuality's respective desires clearly implies understanding men and women, tacitly and explicitly, with regard to their respective self-devotions. It can also be safely assumed, until science proves otherwise, that every human is the result of a heterosexual encounter and, thus, is composed of variable proportions of both sexualities even on a physiological and anatomical level. In other words, every human is both feminine and masculine, masculine and feminine. In short, trying to understand the significance of man's sexualities implies understanding man. The era, or time, in which we live can be characterized by the lack thereof: man is always short on time and can be described as a lack of (his own) time for reasons related to his need to assert himself as a free and rational individual who is equal to all others (asexual) and who is incessantly capable of calculating the conditions that will ideally lead to the optimal and maximum satisfaction of his desires as well as avoiding all inconvenience—including that of his death. The importance of such a struggle is without a doubt inherently central in the message handed down from generation to generation as to the ultimate goal of education. All things considered, the crux of this message is one to every child that he must be perfect: "you will be perfect" means, in other words "you will understand your place in the world" and "you will overcome my own fears, failures, and weaknesses so as to accomplish my desire to be part of this world. This desire which inhabits me has been passed down by my ancestors who, in turn, were informed by their ancestors." Striving for perfection (in other words striving for success) is a characteristic inherent to all humans. For some time it has been exacerbated by the underlying assumption that, through mediation, man can control nature or fortune. This desire is perpetuated by the sense of urgency felt by all humans who for generations have silently and thoughtlessly repeated the neuroses of their mothers and fathers. This desire inhibits man's capacity to listen, to wait and to let flow those feelings that occur when he opens his eyes: in other words limiting the extent to which he feels obligated, to be indebted with fear for the right to live, he opens his heart. Man's capacity to accept the Being, to open himself to It, is *the* fundamental question according to Heidegger: left to its own devices, asexual, virile life tends to undermine the process by which man is paradoxically destined to bloom. At stake is the all but secondary, ontological understanding of man's sexualities.

Notes

1. The notion of "nature" is meaningless to Judaism—cf for example the comment by Léo Strauss in *Natural Right and History*, chapters III & IV (University of Chicago Press, Chicago, 1953).
2. Cf however the second version of Genesis, *Gn*, 1, 20–23.
3. Orthodox in the original sense of the word, not in the theological, history or geographical sense.
4. *Métaphysics*, 1072b, 15 and s. ; cf *Nicomachean Ethics*, 1177a, 15–30.
5. Cf Buber M., "Eastern Spirit and Judaïsm," in *On Judaïsm* (New York, Shoken Books, 1967).
6. The contemplative Greek approach is characterized in this way. See n. 4 of this chapter.
7. Cf Kojève A., "L'origine chrétienne des sciences modernes," *Mélanges Alexandre Koyré II*, Paris, 1964.

8 Descartes, *Meditations on First Philosophy*, Fourth meditation; comp. Third meditation, and the *Discourse on the Method*, Part IV.
9 The notion of post-modernity still seeking, in sometimes dramatic fashion, its meaning, will remain unexplored for the moment.
10 No matter how the reader chooses to consider the following schema, from top to bottom or vice versa, the purpose is to define a clear reference point.
11 *Infra,* Part III.
12 Understanding that the human individual is the principle object of study here, it will be easier and less effusive to use the terms masculine and feminine in isolation except when of man is necessary for clarity.

Part II
The Sexes

> The natural impulse or desire, which Hobbes attributes to mankind of subduing one another, is far from being well founded.
>
> Next to a sense of his weakness, man would soon find himself sensible of his wants. Hence another law of nature would prompt him to seek for nourishment.
>
> Fear, I have observed, would incline men to shun one another; but the marks of this fear being reciprocal would soon induce them to associate. Besides, this association would quickly follow from the very pleasure one animal feels at the approach of another of the same species. Again, the attraction arising from the difference of sexes would enhance this pleasure, and the natural inclination they have for each other, would form a third law.[1]

Recognizing the pressing importance of characterizing the masculine and feminine within man may seem like an untimely exercise at the very least. Yet doing so will permit a better understanding of humanity at a time when differences between the sexes are believed to be insignificant in both man's ability to understand the world as well as in his quest for leading a fulfilling existence. However, recognizing these differences serves the purposes of a masculine ideology to the detriment of a legitimate recognition of women's role in society, culture and education. Before revealing the interaction, burden and crossroads of meaning to which these differences give way, in part by alluding to the past and future intertwining of paganism and Judaism, it is apposite to reveal what is at stake by doing so. Such is the objective of this part of our book.

The analysis of the phenomenology of human sexuality (Part II) will be carried out by revealing a certain number of political issues that will then be addressed in the third part of this book.

4
Fractal Morals

Abstract: *This chapter introduces the further parallel between feminine and Judaism on one hand, and masculine and paganism, on the other. It does so presenting a defence of feminism, which illustrates and makes progressively real, the unhurried worldwide equalization of male and female rights and political capacities. Feminism may be understood as the genuine core stake of the current globalization dynamic. Discussing the relations between psychology and politics, this chapter insists on the not only relevant but necessary parallel between the smallest (e.g. individuals) and the biggest—our whole world—with respect to our most important problems. In this horizon, sexuality and globalization echo each other.*

Keywords: *feminine; feminism; masculine; psychology; politics; sexuality*

Bibard, Laurent. *Sexuality and Globalization: An Introduction to a Phenomenology of Sexualities.* New York: Palgrave Macmillan, 2014.
DOI: 10.1057/9781137469298.0010.

Three inseparable observations have hereto been made: (1) the contemporary predominance of economics on the intellectual and practical facets of life; (2) man's expressly "modern" desire to master his environment; and 3) the recognition of sexuality at the center of man's existence. Until now the focus of this book has been to reveal the relationship between contemporary economism and the modern desire to know as well as to master and to control. There is little question today that sexuality is a driving force for both thought and action within man's individual and collective conscious and subconscious. Various symbols, actions, and realities bear witness to the central role that sexuality plays in today's world: its pervasiveness in advertisements, a dramatic increase worldwide of all forms of pornography and prostitution, and even the associated call for the protection of women, whose image is overexploited, and their dignity. Everyone has a clear interest in sexuality albeit in inconsistent and variable fashion. Whereas women speak rarely of their conquests, men seek every opportunity to boast of theirs—in other words of their male virility. Understood as a social movement with the political aim of defending women's rights to participate as fully as men in what life has to offer (intellectually or practically speaking), feminism is alternately tacitly and explicitly understood as reflective of its constitutive logic: refusing to fall in line with the logic on which feminism bases its legitimacy is tantamount, especially for the male human, to adopting misogynistic or chauvinistic mentalities that tend to favor the archaic, virile domination of which women are the primary victims. Recognizing the entirety of the female existence is amongst the most obvious and urgent, and the least questionable, of man's scientific, moral and political obligations. To this end it is relevant to note that the indispensable effort to fulfill the conditions requisite to an equal recognition of women, in particular on a political level,[2] is taking place during a period in which the recognition of sexual differentiation of humans is irrelevant on both a practical and, moreover, an intellectual level. It is imperative to recognize the difference between men and women for the express purpose of obliterating this very difference: recognizing this difference will shed light on the alienation that women have endured since the dawn of time. Bringing to light women's plight will, in turn, lead to a balancing of the living conditions of both sexes—in other words an expurgation of the undying dominance of man over woman that has been implicitly passed along from generation to generation. Ultimately success will be measured by the revelation and the eventual redemption of woman's lot. Salvation will come when the world recognizes difference and, in spite of it, treats everyone equally in economic, cultural, political, and social terms.

This salvation is not exclusive to woman but rather is that of humanity as a whole including men and children of both sexes: one person's interest is necessarily intertwined with that of others. Men and women, willingly or not, are dependent upon one another for reproduction, for each other's existence as well as for meaning in their respective existences for no other reason than the fact that differentiation establishes a framework for all encounters. Sexuality serves as a particularly fruitful realm of reflection (which, so it seems, has yet to deal with it) as well as of action because it outlines the most universal as well as unique and intimate theme of human existence. Addressing human sexuality implies simultaneously addressing globalization (the macro-reality) and individual psychology (the micro-reality).

Some might say that placing psychology, an analytical field, a methodology, and a science on the same intellectual plane as globalization, a characteristic, contemporary political issue, is absurd if not impossible, and, at any rate, constitutes a fundamental error in logic. It is indeed impossible, shocking even, to analyze diffuse political issues such as terrorism and contemporary warfare (Israel and Palestine, Iraq or even those in sub-Saharan Africa) with the same attention and methods dedicated to the personal or interpersonal issues of society's most fragile individuals who, at some point, will rely on clinical, psychoanalytical or psychotherapeutic treatments. The refusal to consider these issues as stemming from similar, societal questions is a decision made principally by its male members: females are more likely to accept the pertinence of a psychological approach to human or even political affairs. Men less readily admit that "high-level politics" can be subject to a psychological analysis. To them, "real" politics is grounded in noble or human interest, and therefore transcends the niggling and hair splitting of psychology: "real" politics is always "high" politics. Held to the highest standards of its defining ambition, politics is the means by which man affirms and defends the highest esteem that he, universally speaking, holds of himself. In no event can politics be held hostage to a psychological understanding of man: doing so would cast man in a light that, at best, would make a mockery of him and, at worst, defile him by revealing his eccentricities. Aside from the complexity inherent in a psychological approach to understanding politics, examining globalization and individual psychology from the same analytical framework presents a challenge to both common sense and logic. At first glance it is clearly counterintuitive to claim that universal (globalization) and individual psychology are coextensive. If we accept that the macro unit is "the planet" and that the micro unit is the single individual, logic would have it that the "planet" faces problems on a scale that have no application to those of any individual. It would be an insurmountable task to apply the same metrics used for evaluating global issues such as poverty, the environmental degradation of the planet, economic warfare and increasingly common terrorist attacks to individual issues such as outsourcing of a local business, the drying up of a local river that furnishes the village with water, a poorly remunerated job, and childhood trauma caused by a nearby war. There is no common yardstick for measuring the dimensions, the stakes and the semantic descriptors implied by these two very different constructs and for good reason: on an intermediate—mesoscopic—level there are a number of players that intervene in global and individual issues: the State, media, businesses and many other structures, processes and organizations that mediate the collision of two, incommensurable elements: planet and man.

It seems obvious that these two planes are echoes of one another. Sexuality is simultaneously the most intimate and the most universal element of life in this world and, according to the postulate of this book, constitutes the framework proper to both elements. Analyzing sexuality implies analyzing the totality of human life today. In one way or another, sexuality is the central, contemporary theme of all thought that seeks nowadays to confront head on the entirety of its time. Our approach, in this context, allows for an initially analogical understanding of the world in which we live today. In a modern sense, our approach takes on a mythical allure since it acknowledges not only the possibility for but also, out of respect for its object, the necessity of analyzing the sum of its constitutive parts within the same framework. This framework is all-encompassing as it mediates straightaway the non-inferential connections between the elements that make up our world and others.[3]

This assertion is further muddled by the assertion that thought and action converge even if their respective processes are not the same.

* * *

Seeking to place men and women on the same footing, thereby conferring equality to the sexes, especially in the political world, the feminist movement implicitly recognizes the difference between man and woman by postulating that women are by default subject to an archaic, male domination. The differences between man and woman, initially animalistic before becoming socially and culturally constructed, lack an ontological or "natural" foundation. A world in which reality conforms to "nature" is one in which man and woman are equal, even before the law, be it from the point of view of those who are subject to the laws or of those who write them. Expecting that humans will manifest their true nature implies conceiving a world in which men and women are equal in all respects and in which there is a proclivity for appreciating equality amongst its citizens even in biological terms. Anatomical and physiological differences are, in fact, meaningless in such a world that tends to be exclusively cultural or conceived with the express objective of conclusively eradicating the archaically imagined blueprint of an original, male-dominated world. In line with man's veritably natural state, the true world in which man and woman are equal is conceived as a counterweight to the erroneous constructions of male domination of the species and its ruins. This struggle is apposite to man's salvation. The contemporary world can be characterized by women's overdue right to express themselves, a right that is composed of her claim on a legitimate recognition of all women by men. Recognition of the human species' feminine, by both men and women, means granting an equal role to women in the public realm. Even if women have always held their place in the economics of their home, they have nonetheless been prohibited from participating publicly in intellectual and political spheres. The current era is one in which women must lay claim to their place in the public, political and even intellectual spheres. Claiming their rightful place in the public sphere comes after a long period of silence and implies according the utmost importance to woman's first speech: ushering in unforeseeable worlds, this discourse is but the beginning.

This claim holds true only if the difference between men and women remains as if the distance between the sexes, on the ontological, social and cultural level, had never been breached. If credence is given to the idea that all humans are the fruit of a heterosexual encounter, excluding the possibility of a biotechnological revolution, and that all humans are therefore masculine and feminine in nature, it is illogical to suggest that the feminine, (woman) has never been heard nor ever governed. Making such a claim does little to resolve the central political issue constituted by the marginalization of women in the public, intellectual (theoretical and artistic) and political spheres. It does, however, steer attention toward a question that unifies under a single thought process, the presupposed contradictions posed by feminism with regard to the "naturalist" and "culturalist" positions. If it is assumed that the masculine and feminine are not qualitatively similar, every individual, regardless of his anatomical sex, is both feminine and masculine and therefore possesses both sexualities. If this assumption is correct, human sexualities are dynamically contradictory and thereby fertile for one another. Every human being is "by nature" the product of a sexual meshing that is just as fundamentally incomplete as it is inherent: incomplete because it is the result of an event that is itself contradictory in process and inherent because it is constitutive. In other words every individual, though bi-sexual, is naturally either more woman or man and therefore host to a contradiction that develops as both a brake and glue. It is in the human being's nature to cultivate itself. Despite the staying power of certain archaisms, a result of a slowly, deftly and profoundly imbedded domination, humanity is still malleable even if not forthrightly so. It is still the fruit of an imbroglio between an acquired and innate structure as well as a cultural and natural process. Accepting that man is both home to as well as the result of a bountiful difference between the masculine and the feminine is tantamount to recognizing said difference and opens the door to endless human combinations. Within every individual an incessant combination can be played using the terms masculine, feminine, woman and man, as each of these is innate in man.

The innate and the ultimate encounter of which man is capable is one with and within himself that plays out in the form of a mediation between his dual sexualities. "The natural impulse or desire" which Hobbes attributes to mankind of subduing one another, is far from being well founded.

> ...Fear, I have observed, would incline men to shun one another; but the marks of this fear being reciprocal would soon induce them to associate. Besides, this association would quickly follow from the very pleasure one animal feels at the approach of another of the same species. Again, the attraction arising from the difference of sexes would enhance this pleasure, and the natural inclination they have for each other, would form a third law.[4]

* * *

The three guiding principles hereto examined are: (1) the rapport between the universal and the individual or intimate, (2) *via* the underlying question of recognition, the rapport between identity and difference, and (3) finally the relationship between masculine and feminine on the one hand and men and women on the other, that implies an examination of the relationship between the notions of "nature" and "culture". The underlying question of recognition (2) is the most significant and fundamental to the relationship between the two sexualities: seemingly more politically neutral for their logical (1) and metaphysical (3) qualities, the two other combinations are seemingly more straightforward. These two refer indirectly to the analysis of the contemporary reign of the desire to control, on the one hand, and that of time on the other.

Before associating Judaism to the feminine and paganism to the masculine, and then giving credence to the outcomes of bridging the two, it is important to characterize each of the sexualities in isolation and according to its own logic before comparing one to the other.

Notes

1 Montesquieu, *The Spirit of the Laws*, Book I, chapter II., *The Spirit of the Laws*, Thomas Nugent (trans.) (New York: Macmillan, 1949).
2 In terms of the totality of the practical existence of men and women—cf the characterization by Aristotle of political life (*Nicomachean Ethics*, 1094a25–1094b5), a characterization which, despite the domination of politics by economics alluded to earlier, has not fallen out of favor.
3 The mathematical image of discourse analysis is often useful for clarifying the method employed. We are postulating that the world has a more fractal allure than analogical one (for a clearer and more sober description of this notion, cf Ian Stewart, *Does God Play Dice? The New Mathematics of Chaos*, chapter 11 (Blackwell Publishing, 2002)).
4 Montesquieu, *The Spirit of the Laws*, Book I, chapter II.

5
Interlacings

Abstract: *The feminine and masculine sexualities are here presented in a phenomenological perspective as spontaneously vitalized toward their self-actualization. Against the Freudian perspective, the feminine is not considered here on the basis of the lack of a penis. It is on the contrary considered on the basis of the girl's certainty of being able, like her mother, to reproduce. Feminine is synonymous with identity, while masculine is associated with difference; the masculine, on the other hand, begins with the sentiment of being rejected from the innately perfect world of the mother's womb. How feminine and masculine look for their self-actualization through meeting each other is made clear in the context of pre-Christian sexualities' further transformations.*

Keywords: *desire; difference; identity; interlacing; feminine; masculine*

Bibard, Laurent. *Sexuality and Globalization: An Introduction to a Phenomenology of Sexualities.* New York: Palgrave Macmillan, 2014.
DOI: 10.1057/9781137469298.0011.

Feminine

A young girl purportedly feels a sense of deprivation with regard to the opposite sex. At least on an anatomical level the absence of the male genitalia is clear. Implicitly understood prior to the advent of psychoanalysis the explicit hypothesis that psychoanalysis posits with regard to virile strength has been generally accepted since. In this chapter, however, the distinction between masculine and feminine will be approached differently: from generation to generation, young girls, whether ultimately they do so or not, are assured the possibility of following in their mothers' footsteps by carrying unborn children and bringing them into the world. This set cycle places every female child in an essential, intergenerational continuity whose origins are forever lost in time immemorial. The paradigm of feminine identity is posited on the simple observation of the continuity, from generation to generation, of woman's role in bringing into existence those who are born. The certainty of existence, ensured by heterosexual encounter, constitutes the dynamic origins of the feminine. That such a statement is hardly if ever uttered should not diminish its veracity: its reality is more powerful than any words. The feminine's place in this world is thus secured by the human race's reliance on her for perpetuation: the ability to sustain life is requisite to perpetuating life from generation to generation. Without ever the slightest doubt, existing and providing for existence are one and the same.[1] The numerous ways in which man fulfills his vital needs are in his distant past: in the present, man is innately working to satisfy his fundamental needs in one way or another. The way in which he does so is intrinsic: he is characteristically identified as living in a certain way to the extent that imagining another is outright impossible. Any "other" way is, in fact, insignificant because it cannot be conceived as a means of survival. Any challenge to my conviction in the nullity of an alternate way, would by definition stand in opposition to my existence whose certainty is grounded in the assertion of the truth—the lone truth. Even when challenged by a different means of existence, my truth is above all practical as it fulfills my immediate needs, thereby discrediting the alternate method and furthermore revealing that it represents a fundamental lapse with regard to what is necessary for getting things done and *done* well. It is understood that he who operates differently than I is mistaken; it is impossible for me to imagine things otherwise. The aforementioned lapse is, in practical terms, evil. Such is my reality, above all else faithful to the routine that assures my existence from one day to the next. I, woman, am the continuation of my mother, an identity that transcends generations, a renewal of itself and which, in the contemporaneity of families, clans, villages, and peoples establishes a relationship between good and evil that is analogous to the rapport of identity to difference.

Psychoanalysis' aforementioned hypothesis is nevertheless sooner or later applicable: at the heart of that which defines the community into which I was born, to which I belong and in which difference is a defining element in the form of that which I am not, is the feminine's "other": the masculine. The masculine is not in this case an enemy combatant but rather a difference that is integral to my community. That which is evil, flawed, error-prone, alterity itself constitutes the core of the "other" although the latter is not simply conceived as such. This is the "other" that can be found *as* "the other" contributing to its own security and longevity, and thus to mine. Another reality constitutes the dynamic that binds me to the "other" where the identity of my community is concerned: physically speaking he is at least, at first glance, superior to me, woman, and more capable than I am of demarcating his territory, resisting enemy threat and capturing sought after prey. My identity cannot therefore stand alone and can only preserve its nature by implicating the other who is continually reassuring and reaffirming. The community that identifies itself by territory and by the perpetuation of generations is, by construction, heterosexual. The other heterosexual is responsible for defending and protecting me as well as assuring the fluid continuity of the generations. It is clear to me that my community will one day face a genuine threat and that living means confronting this world's many dangers: animal and human predators, cataclysms, disease, etc. The greatest dangers nevertheless come from within my community: sooner or later disagreement will reveal the potential deterioration of the certainty upon which my identity is constructed. Even more troublesome is the fact that the destabilization of my identity is a result of the very sentiment at the heart of that which defines my being: that which is different, fallible, error-prone and evil. What is most surprising and most painful is realizing that in the same space in which I gain the confidence that allows my existence as a woman to perpetuate the species also takes root an alterity that is an evil menace, failure, error, and struggle. My place is sooner or later less certain than it seemed when my existence was initially defined in practice. Such disillusionment is potentially ubiquitous since I know that my community's survival is dependent upon its ability to defend itself from predators, disease, and cataclysm. In due course I will recognize the tenuousness of the identity that defines my existence but will not let that realization impede me from knowing that I know. The latter act is possible because I possess a know-how that encompasses that which I have yet to do but that I will learn to do. Central to the torment that danger and increasing uncertainty are ubiquitous, I defend the certitude of existence. I am this very defense and existence, and exist by the very act of defending it: I do so by using existence as an active player in its own defense. I validate myself through my experience; I have no other evidence and do not require any. This truth, my truth, serves as the foundation for my survival, is sufficient for doing so, and constitutes the backbone of my struggle against difference. It is inimitable, active, and is nourished by a sensational sentiment that stimulates me to experience myself as a living, resisting affirmation of myself without needing further commentary about the fact that I am holding out or about "persisting in my own being."

Should it be necessary, for whatever the reason, that I ensure this dual certainty, one thing is undisputable: the reality of its action in me and as myself. This reality is not voluntary on my part: it simply is. I am aware of it even if I do not explicitly choose it. I clearly enjoy it, enjoying my existence on Earth, and assuring that my ancestors and children, as well as their children, do the same. It is the ultimate foundation for the affirmation of my existence. I could perhaps give it thanks, be grateful for this dual certainty that allows me to survive in the storm of torment. In which case I would also be thanking something that I cannot name and of which I am only the living, sentimental result. I am not responsible for its existence but rather something else; it is something radically different. Different than me, different than anyone else, an alterity that is not unknown and enemy but evasive and paradoxically shrouded in me, and therefore a friend that is fundamentally favorable to my existence. "Something" is at work within me that sustains me by feeding my own resistance. This thing cannot be articulated by way of ordinary language, or the practical language that determines the exchange of resources in and ideas about our world; it is therefore rarely articulated. Rather it is seen, recognized, and corroborated by practice in the everyday world. Because I exist at the heart of this very dynamic, I know that I am capable of anything—that I am resilient, and that although I may one day die at the hands of another I can nonetheless take on any challenge because I measure up to everything. As a result of the reinforced certainty of my being and my identity, I am capable of confronting, and anxious to do so, that which I am not, the other, the differences and perhaps even doubt! Such desire and doubt originate from the fact that evil one day came to be part of that which was originally the only living whole of my existence. Despite the immeasurable pain, I continued to resist and constructed my identity as a repeated affirmation of myself as a being amongst an infinite variety of others. The difference that I once feared and inherently believed to be unhealthy then became a part of me. Rather than threatening me, this identical, fundamental truth comes to reassure me in my existence and renders me ever more capable of handling the differences in the world that were not originally a part of me—all subconsciously. So here I am true to myself because I am differentiated from myself and able to be so because I have persevered in the identity that I have encapsulated from the beginning because it is a part of me.

The feminine, originally the established identity certain of being the intergenerational perpetuator of the generations, finds its true power to the extent that it opens itself to difference, otherness, and threats, either seeming or real, to its being. Based on the certainty that constitutes its being, the feminine must persist in its existence by encapsulating its foil that remains unknown—without ceasing to do so as long as it lives.

Masculine

For the masculine, birth is an act during which he is expelled from a world where everything is provided: he is anything but the immediate recreation of being part of a perpetuated cycle as was his mother. He is essentially an outsider. Given that his birth brought an end to his Omni-existence, it also means that his initial existence is tantamount to not being, no longer being, and having lost the foundation upon which his being was guaranteed. From the very beginning desire is central to the masculine's existence. He is defined as the absence of his own origin. When he remembers the space from which he was expelled, he yearns to find his place, a place that he may never find. The masculine is born as a test of want, and an obligation to create his place in a world where he otherwise would not have one.

In his quest to find his place, the masculine cannot rely on his origins because, once he was expelled from there, he was expelled for life: once and for all.[2] Supposing that he pursues his journey, the masculine is defined by the quest for his place in a world that, by construction, will accept him in the same way that he was received at the moment of his conception but without allowing for the possibility that he be yet again expelled from his world. The world he seeks is necessarily stable and unchanging if we assume that instability and change are synonymous with expulsion and rejection. Given the basis of his sentiments of rejection, doubt, and uncertainty that are a result of his own origins, the masculine seeks reception, certainty, and settling down into a world and as a world. "As a world" given that the individual identity that constitutes him was a failure. The world that the masculine seeks for and as himself is the world he seeks for the future. He imagines himself as being intensely mundane to the point that he considers himself as being the place where he would want to be received. In the strictest definition of the terms, he desires to be self-mobile and autonomous in order to assure his own respite.

Contrary to the feminine, far from seeking out and accepting alterity, the masculine, itself born of the other, difference, and therefore "thrown out" of its identity, seeks similarity, himself as identity. He seeks an identity that will not push him into the alterity that he experienced when brought into the "world." The space sought out by the masculine is by definition a stable identity that, if impeded from being transformed into its other or into difference, is a synonym of eternity. Time to the masculine is synonymous with the inherent evil in which his identity finds source as an inherent absence on a quest to fulfill itself. To the feminine space was what it needed (willingly or not) to escape. By doing so the feminine only reaffirmed its identity. In fulfilling itself, the masculine tends to halt the movement that brings it closer to itself—for doing so is painful, whereas the feminine tends to feed the aforementioned differences that strengthen it and reaffirm its existence—and this without hesitation.

The "world" sought out by the masculine is by construction without beginning or end: it is not supposed to be dependent on the individual wishes of any one person. The autonomous authority that the masculine seeks for itself as a complete receptiveness is never a result of the inherent failure that brought him to his reality. On the contrary, this stable, for eternal world in which the masculine is absorbed, thereby losing his inherent shortcomings, reabsorbs itself as an inherently insufficient being and encompasses the entirety of all possible, ontological shortcomings. For if these shortcomings are not initially understood to be absorbed and thus overcome by way of their inclusion how, given the radicality of doubt that the masculine is, can we imagine advancing toward a sensible future? On what other basis can we humans, having experienced the absence of any basis to begin with, find traction if not upon the belief that the sentiment of being nothing, or being a negation is intrinsically positioned with regard to our blissful abolition? Teleology is inherent in the masculine when the latter seeks reassurance, an eventual and identical affirmation of its own identity. This is the only way of recognizing oneself in the other: born as "the other," in other words as myself, I only recognize myself in others to the extent that they are on the same quest as I am on, that of ease, identity, of similarity, of the truth, with the understanding that their quest is not based upon the life into which we were born. Born as difference, the masculine is teleologically oriented toward a transcendent space that represents, symbolizes, and brings to reality its ease as a (re)conquered identity.

Finally, since one such world is transcendent, it is clearly absurd to expect one day an interaction with it in any way other than by the most absolute receptivity possible. The accomplished version of the masculine seeks to be as porous as possible, entirely open without wanting to transform the world around him, "theoretical" in the pure, original meaning of the word, "mindfulness."

Chiasmus

The masculine and the feminine are paradoxically reunited at the springboard of the desire that orients them, in one way or another, beyond the immediacy of the world in which they come to be. The feminine is driven toward otherness and the masculine toward an identity that is understood as qualitatively differentiated from life itself and in which he is above all the negation of himself. If humanity is considered an artifice, it is masculine in origin as it is excluded from the living spontaneity from which it originates. Even if humanity can be considered a natural occurrence, it becomes the act of emerging from and surpassing the identity or sameness by which it is first felt in nature and in order to become reality through words.

The ensemble of the preceding propositions suggests that sooner or later the fates of the masculine and the feminine will meet within man. Independent of its own will, and even then if only to maintain the *status quo*, the feminine, understood as initial identity or "sameness," is a continual opening toward the other. The masculine, on the other hand, understood as initially different with regard to his origins and thus with himself, the "other" as a distortion constituted as an abrupt transition, seeks to complete himself or his difference as identity or as "sameness" that he finally acquires. At every instance each sex is vectored toward its other: the feminine finds difference in the masculine whereas the masculine seeks identity in the feminine. However, the way in which each sex perceives itself does not correlate directly to that which it wants from the other, but rather is one step out of phase in terms of the internal dynamic that defines its existence. The alterity sought out by the feminine is not satisfied by the "other" males and the differences that constitute their community any more than the identity sought out by the masculine is satisfied by the "sameness" that women pass down from generation to generation. During the courting process, at their first nuptial encounter each of the sexes believes for some time that its partner will immediately satisfy the core of his expectations when in reality the interlacing that will bring the sexes together and eventually into conflict for having believed one another is just commencing. The other sex is always, and only, for the other the space where their respective desires take root. Their encounter becomes meaningful only when the realms and languages capable of facilitating the exchange of their expectations is discovered without either party being judged by the other or by itself for feelings of disappointment, deceit, or having knowingly or not been unfaithful to the other. Whether or not humanity in general accepts it, sexuality is the space in which wars, lives, love, and peace emerge, take shape, and die. It constitutes the space in which man's agreements and misunderstandings are forged.

It will be useful to present clearly the sexes' respective, constitutive elements:

The feminine in its inherent state is:

- Identity (*sameness* as a continuation of the living)
- Certainty
- Practical or active prominence
- *Rapport* or collectivity
- Intractable with regard to otherness that is not included by default

The masculine in its inherent state is:

- Difference (alterity by virtue of being an alteration)
- Regret, disquiet, doubt
- "Theoretical" questioning of the world he seeks that is, by construction, *beyond* the practical evidence of the world in which he lives
- Isolated individual
- Paradoxical search for any possible identity

What the feminine seeks to become:

- Differentiation
- Combined fear and desire
- "Theoretical" questioning of the world sought above and beyond the practical evidence of the world in which it lives
- Individualization
- Paradoxical search for any possible *new* identity

What the masculine seeks to become:

- Identity (sameness identified as *eternal*)
- Truth
- Theoretical acceptance of the source of all action
- A meaningful whole (world)
- Intractable with regard to alterity persisting as such

Placing the four states of being face to face results in the following

* * *

It is within reason to say that the masculine in its inherent state lines up with that which the feminine seeks to be and vice versa. There remain, however, a few nuances to be brought to light that are decisive in this analysis and that nourish the aforementioned misunderstandings. Opposite the feminine's existence, certainty, and practical being are juxtaposed the masculine's eternity, truth and theoretical being. As a counterbalance to the masculine's difference, isolation, regret and inborn uniqueness are the feminine's individualizing differentiation, fearful desire, and uncertainty. The masculine's ability to reflect theoretically upon the world propels the feminine toward her freedom; the feminine's innate ability to calmly and efficiently live in the world and as the world propels man to his existence. Foremost theoretical (Greek), the masculine's energy is centripetal to an active and or practical end. Above all practical, the feminine's energy is centrifugal to a theoretical end. Each sex shelters that which the other seeks for itself which is deformed by the complex prisms that constitute their inherently dynamic origins.

Not only does each sex represent, symbolize, and evoke the vital force of the other which is the object of its desire, but it is also the catalyst for its dynamic force. The physical force of the male body contributes to the efficiency of the processes by which a community ensures its survival whereas the woman's desirable receptivity makes possible a contemplative esthetic that respects the nature of all things that mysteriously produces self-reflecting and verbally communicative existence.

* * *

Presented in this way, the two sexes and their respective spontaneity can be described as pre-modern: with neither the intention nor the explicit and systematic attempt to control the outcomes of man's action on the world. The respective attempts to master and control these effects can be described as each sex's "virilities." The virile masculine forces his imagined desire for identity whereas the virile feminine demonstrates her openness to new things by way of its practical use of all knowledge. The ultimate test by which the masculine will intrude on the world is his fight to the death by which he will cunningly transgress the temporal limits of life in order to prove his existence. To a certain extent, such a life holds nothing for the masculine that seeks to demonstrate his eternity. The ultimate test by which the feminine imposes nature, which is its original identity, upon itself is the work founded upon knowledge upon which nature over-"natures" itself. Nature as such holds nothing for the feminine that seeks difference.

The masculine and virile battle is ultimately the political test of war. The ultimate test of feminine mastery is ultimately that of technical and productive sciences as well as the exchanges that take place in a modern economy.

TABLE 5.1   *Chiasma of the Sexes*

The feminine in its inherent state is:	What the masculine seeks to become:
• Identity (*sameness* as a continuation of the living) • Certainty • Practical or active prominence • *Rapport* or collectivity • Intractable with regard to otherness that is not included by default	• Identity (sameness identified as *eternal*) • Truth • Theoretical acceptance of the source of all action • A meaningful whole (world) • Intractable with regard to alterity
The masculine in its inherent state is:	What the feminine seeks to become:
• Difference (alterity by virtue of being an alteration) • Regret, disquiet, doubt • "Theoretical" questioning of the world he seeks that is, by construction, *beyond* the practical evidence of the world in which he lives • Isolated individual • Paradoxical search for any possible identity	• Differentiation • Combined fear and desire • "Theoretical" questioning of the world sought above and beyond the practical evidence of the world in which it lives • Individualization • Paradoxical search for any possible *new* identity

Notes

1 The frenzied development of varied scientific domains such as ethology, paleontology, etc undermine in no way certain observations concerning man that demonstrate the necessity, in order for human life to continue, for parents to take particular care of their children. The modern effacement of the difference between man and animal, as a function of the impersonal development of the objective sciences of the living, does not undermine the ontological question of the rapport between the human and the animalistic.

2 Cf Hegel, *Lectures on the Philosophy of Religion* (Oxford University Press, 2007). II, 2), quoted by Bourgeois B., "La déraison historique," in *Etudes hégéliennes, Raison et décision*, PUF, 1992, p. 284.

6
Drama

Abstract: *This chapter presents some political consequences of the parallel between the feminine and Judaism, on one hand, and masculine and paganism, on the other hand. Doing so, it makes clear the relevance of comparing the "smallest" or the individual level approached on the basis of the gender issue, and the "biggest," or worldwide history, considered in the horizon of the Western tension between its two determining roots. As feminine and masculine are fulfilled in an ambivalent way through their partial transformation into their "other," so are Judaism and paganism. Before Christianity, such interlacing radically changed neither the feminine nor the masculine, nor the human world.*

Keywords: *Christianity; feminine; Judaism; masculine; paganism; politics*

Bibard, Laurent. *Sexuality and Globalization: An Introduction to a Phenomenology of Sexualities.*
New York: Palgrave Macmillan, 2014.
DOI: 10.1057/9781137469298.0012.

The idea that Greek paganism and Judaism demonstrate and confirm respectively masculine and feminine characteristics of humanity implies that the "West," defined as the explicit affirmation and institutionalization of political, scientific and technical means as well as the control and possession of human and non-human nature, is the outcome of a given interlacing of the two. This interlacing was earlier described as the Christian subsumption, supposedly definitive in light of its absolute character, of paganism by Judaism. In theological terms the subsumed is the "nature" that structures Greek paganism. It is subsumed by the Jewish notion of divinity that is de facto transformed into the Judeo-Christian notion of a god that is raised from the dead because, at a given time and place, though for eternity and for the entire universe, he died on the Cross. It remains to be seen to what extent such a transformative subsumption is a result of the subsumption of man's masculine to his feminine that results in the virilization of both.

* * *

Paganism was earlier characterized as being centered on the notion of nature. It is Plato who produces the most complete, pagan explanation of the effects of bridging "nature" with "culture" or "convention." His explanation is systematically organized around the question of knowing how men could live together in a satisfactory way. The relationship of the conflict between nature and culture is seemingly political and, given the importance of nature in pagan culture, the problem of nature's relationship to culture is paramount. The prominence given to the notion of equilibrium and to its contrary, *hubris* is evident: the act of exceeding the equilibrium, or "natural" measure of all things. *Hubris*, which can include the ideals of culture or even arbitrary convention, is fundamentally contrary to the ideals of nature. If "nature" is ultimately all encompassing, that means that it also includes that which transgresses natural law (subject to scientific understanding) including culture and convention. The latter are therefore the possessions of nature itself: Christianity which subsumes nature through "culture," convention or will, claims the exact opposite of this hypothesis. Rather, it affirms that "nature" is the result of culture or desire. "Knowing" is above all a gift given to man by God: man's "natural" enlightenment is sooner or later the result of divine grace. According to the pagan connotation of the word, however, the entirety of the political issue is of a natural order. The problem with politics is that humans are not able to agree on the means to an end, in this case living together in harmony, and that their disagreement is sooner or later a result of their desire to surpass the natural limit of that which is possible. All political problems are a result of man's persistent desire to have more than he already has for his own satisfaction: desire is the tyrant.[1] The political problem par excellence can be summarized by the scarcity of objects that stimulate desire, in other words, the limit of man's energy. Successful politics can be defined as that which is able to restrain desire within the limits of reasonable balance; this is politics as a discipline and as human action.[2] But before restraining desire within the limits of natural equilibrium, the latter has to be understood: only the wise understand it and wisdom is a prerequisite to governing. Man is not born a sage but rather moved by desire, lacking all control, and therefore the exact opposite of wise. Governing aptly implies that wise men do exist and therefore that education is possible.[3] Education is a spontaneous element of "nature" as is the entrenchment of mankind's offspring in the corruption, convention or transgression of the laws of nature by nature or desire. It is just as natural to want to conform to nature as it is to try to break with it.

Trying to break with nature is more understandably inherent to man given that one such derogation is an integral characteristic of nature: the act of bringing the male child to life is one example.[4] The masculine phenomenon of humanity represents, in its being, the possibility that man break with "nature" since he is, before desiring to be so, the very event of being "expelled" from nature, assuming that the mother symbolizes nature, her womb, the nascent space that is archaic, indomitable and constitutively more vast than any thought. It is also just as natural to be masculine—cultural, conventional, arbitrary, disoriented, absurd—as it is to be feminine—natural, immediate, spontaneous, necessary, vectored, sensible. The primary problem with the political is the rapport between the masculine and feminine within man: the first reveals the possibility of disorder to the second. The masculine must "look after" itself according to the feminine's rules. Two examples, taken from the Greek tradition, support this hypothesis: the mother of Socrates who became prideful through her work and the woman who drove Parmenides' chariot. The feminine is the salvation of man whose disorientation is masculine in origin; women are only disoriented as a result of masculine disorientations. That said, women are not instantly man's salvation: to the contrary, it is after leaving them that men are first unwise or non-existent, whereas women are born being. Men are born unwise, an absence of wisdom that is constitutive and that "naturally" defines them as philosophers (*philo-sophia*), preoccupied with the idea of that which they are born without, wisdom or conformity to nature. Philosophy is the ultimate truth of Greek paganism. It begins with astonishment, the very notion of that which is found "unnatural," the discovery of nature begins with the feeling that "something" is not as it should be, or as an intuition that it should be. The normative is inscribed in the classical notion of "nature" that encompasses the idea of "natural right." Having, or believing to have an intuition with regard to the way that things should happen in order to conform to their nature implies that intuition is at work even in the man having gone astray. In the same space in which nature dismisses man in his original state, it is also working spontaneously, simultaneously or naturally to understand itself. The possibility of surprise and doubt in man is made possible by the energy differential between dismissal and intuition. This possibility is made clear through philosophy which can be defined as the natural pursuit of wisdom. Nature leads man astray of himself so as to find its own identity and fulfill itself within man's body: this much is clear in Aristotle's *Metaphysics*.[5] In pagan terms, wisdom means contemplating the absolute. It is seeking identity in the absolute, where identity is a fragile process dependent on the conditions of man's material existence.[6] Ideally the sage's relationship with nature, as with man, is unbridled and unearthly since he is the unifying identity of *one*, the unifying principle according to which all things are sensed, are experienced, are part of a unified whole. Beginning with the moment that he consciously identifies with all, the sage is no longer a single individual but rather thought which thinks itself in absolute terms. The success of the individual's pursuit of meaning is tantamount to the abolition of differentiated individuality that has always been perceived by the masculine as a failure. When the body becomes the ultimate object of reflection, the masculine reveals itself as a failure. The body is the terrain where absence, regret, and deficiency are felt. Only after meeting his vital needs can man, liberated, begin to rise to his truth, to try to meet his destiny which is to think of the world in which he lives in absolute terms.[7]

For Greek pagans, the body is symbolically and practically represented, in and by philosophy, by the feminine: Socrates brought souls to being whereas his mother brought bodies to being. At the outset, philosophy was understood by voluntarily differentiating between the natural blueprint of the generations and corruption of its living individuals as well as by drawing analogical comparisons to its processes.

It is also the dynamic that allowed paganism, the symbol, matrix and privileged expression of the masculine, to formulate itself. In terms of what can be called the spirit or soul, philosophy seeks that of which the feminine is already capable in this world. Practicing philosophy means using the feminine as a symbol of truth in order to quit the immediate reality and bring forward, in masculine terms of thought, an analogue of its processes. There is a rift between philosophy, the privileged expression of the masculine, and the feminine. Philosophy's attempt to fulfill itself in wisdom is a result of what the feminine's existence reveals to it about the body.[8] Even if women have not traditionally governed, the feminine's archetypal blueprint is political.

Women, left to their own devices, are seen by the masculine as being disoriented, a-human, if not inhuman, and excessive.[9] In order for the political aspect to serve mankind, and in this case the masculine, it must do what it can to control the feminine: the philosophers must govern. One such government must never be imposed, in which case it would then be excessive and irreverent of nature. If nature allows for politics to be removed from its own natural conditions of completing the masculine, it is wise to let it do so and to wait for the opportune time before taking action that will usher in a welcome return of the philosopher king.[10] The nodal means by which politics is synonymous of fulfillment of the masculine is for the former to conform to the latter: teleological in nature, complete, delimited, and identical to himself to the extent possible. In accordance with the search for an identity that defines man, masculine politics is at the very least conservative: innovation which favors the provisional denaturing of the world is, for the masculine, a dangerous operation in political terms. Since on the other hand the masculine understands itself as an absence of identity, or in other words, in political speak, doubting all evidence of the existence of community,[11] it is fundamentally and ontologically speaking excessive—without orientation, without meaning, and without limit. The masculine, left to its own devices, is sub- or supra-human but it is not human—or if he is, only as a frail animal.[12] Excess is inherent in philosophical endeavors whose intrinsic innovation of ideas must be masked from the vision of the politics that it threatens.[13] Philosophers consider politics in an exclusively negative light, as an inevitable terrain requisite to playing out one's own ideas. Greek paganism or man's masculine, is politically conservative and, in the strictest sense of terms, ideologically or metaphysically an anarchist.

Contemporary feminism pertinently characterizes classical politics as antifeminist or chauvinist. Within classical Greek paganism, in which man's masculine characteristics are particularly present, the feminine excess is at work, amicably united by Aristophanes[14] for example.

It goes without saying that excess is an integral part of the Jewish dogma: "God," Yahweh, is the incommensurable gauge of everything. In the Jewish tradition the only gauge is the one that God imposes not only on man but also on the birds of the sky, the fish of the sea and the plants and animals. The ultimate of God's commandments is for man to live up to the highest demands of such an incommensurable gauge: it is therefore his duty. "Living up to" does not suggest being equal to, but simply means believing, submitting oneself without question, having faith, loving and having confidence no matter the circumstances. Even circumstances that plant doubt in man's mind are comprised as they suggest the incomprehensible suffering caused by war, persecution, cataclysms as well as internal strife. There is no method for verifying in truth, in one way or another, my act of faith. Furthermore, my act only has meaning when it persists in its affirmation which is dependent on anything that may cause doubt in me. Its truth is a practical not a theoretical one. In practical terms, anything that seemingly demonstrates that there is nobody, the fact that I believe in nothing when I believe in "God" is transformed into proof of or as a signal of His presence, of His benevolent and infinitely demanding presence. This continual reiteration of my faith is a result of the constitutive sentiment that invigorates the feminine in man. As a symbol of belief, and lacking in any doubt whatsoever, I am its certitude. The mere thought of questioning is foreign to me and anything characterized as "different" is rejected, in the strictest sense of the term, as absurd. I take nothing at face value that does not reflect my nature and of which I am irrefutably certain. I am born as the living entirety of a world that is built to last with the certainty that perpetuating life is a good thing. That which diverges from what I know and live simply does not exist; I give it no credence and am distrustful of it. For, being the very realm of evidence of my being, I know my destiny is to guarantee that life continues after me, and that this is good *per se*. I am also aware of my lack of choice in existence and conviction but rather channel the latter and understand it by analyzing myself. My only autonomy with regard to channeling conviction is remaining open to the possibility of having faith or not.

The most obvious sign of the active presence of an independent force that decides what I must do and think in order for life as I know it to continue is the feeling of an active life within me. Whether I like it or not, I find myself in this world as a woman, the very receptacle of life. "Finding myself here" is not an act of which I alone am capable. Yet this sentiment is capable of muscling its way into me with force and coherence such as I could *not* imagine a person, in the image of myself, yet on an infinitely higher realm of existence, being the author of this very sentiment. My blood is the vehicle of a will that surpasses me infinitely. My nobility, my grandeur, my love or my faith are defined by knowing how to live up to such expectations and to conform humbly in doing so. My ultimate meaning is to grow, to reproduce and to bear witness to my love for my faith by having children who themselves will be fruitful and multiply.

Human men do not understand this thought process. Though they are mistaken, they believe, and sometimes say, that they are the origin of life in women. As is the case for women in whom desire is the catalyst for making things possible, it is not their arbitrary will, infinitely poor compared to the "Author" of all things, that is at work, but rather that of God. Desire is never only sexual; it is God's will in men. And this is so, because the body is never just corporeal or flesh and bones as men or "pagans" sometimes believe: the body is the passage of God in man. The meaning innate in man comes from His will. This certainty, whose origins are in the sentiment of existence as one's self is above all feminine. By way of the certainty that it implies in being, lasting, and ensuring the propagation of man, the feminine body is the premier incarnation of God's will. The ultimate sign of God's active presence in the world that he created is the gestation of woman. This is the human-level manifestation of the act of divine creation which is in itself the here-and-now possibility of human speech that is the infinitely humble yet visible reproduction of the Divine word.[15] By simply opening one's eyes one cannot help but see that meaning is innate to the living body and that enigmatic meaning permeates human sexuality. Deeply ingrained and powerless in the flesh, no idolater is capable of such an understanding. The others, all "others" in the pejorative meaning of the word, are those who do not believe as I do and of which I am living proof. Either the others believe as I do, and participate in my community, as the "same" in which and as which I identify, or, in enemy terms, they are "other." As a final and ultimate judge of the bellicose rapport that I have with non believers, pagans, what I consider "all other," my God is the god of all men even those who do not believe in Him. My "God," the god of all men, is the "all other" because he is neither the same, nor those, including the men in my community, who lower themselves to that level. Nor is he by definition the others who are non believers. All-powerful, sovereign, and absolute, He is the "all other," the entirely inaccessible and therefore "other," creator of everything and myself. Much like a parable, he is conceived as resembling a person because the rapport that I have with others, whoever they may be in the world, is a personal one. It is so because this is the way that I understand myself—sensationally, psychologically, spiritually. Ultimately it is all that I understand. The impersonal character of things as seen by man or by pagans is something that I want neither to access nor to understand.

Whereas the influence of the feminine is perceptible in Greek paganism, the masculine can be seen through the prism of Judaism in the form of the law: I can only imagine meaningful community life insofar as I create synergy between passions and truths which, although similarly driven, are all differentiated and individual. The feminine is the movement toward and a function of difference. Difference for the feminine is fundamentally "otherness" since it is, in short, identity. The "all other," inaccessible by natural means of understanding, is sooner or later the pole by which the feminine orients itself. As long as there is certainty this "all other," which is by construction naturally void of meaning but by way of feeling, certainty or faith can be sought out in many different ways. The feminine, which is defined as openness toward "the other," differs in the way in which it opens itself. Judaism, a historical matrix of the feminine as a religious relationship to a god, is fundamentally and by

TABLE 6.1 *Chiasma of Judaism and Paganism*

Paganism	Judaism
– Originally multiple, tending to a unity or an identity	– Originally one, tending to multiple or to difference
– Ultimately philosophical rapport to nature	– Religious, ultimately theological rapport to "God"
– Man's achievement: total receptivity of all things	– Man's achievement: creative or transformative action analog to divine creation
– "Under" the barometer imposed by law, the feminine *hubris*: Antigone versus Creon.	– "Under" the infinite love for "God," the barometer imposed by law in virile fashion: Moses versus the prophets.

definition pluralistic. The masculine, innately disorientation that seeks direction on the very basis of the difference that it is, exists as convergence particularly in terms of politics and law. Paganism exists in many forms that contradictorily identify themselves as a unique, privileged and exclusive voice.[16]

* * *

When Christianity imposes a new notion of time, independently of its theological dogma, it obscures, perhaps even hides entirely, any comprehension of the original notion of time. It does so as it prepares to subsume paganism to Judaism, of nature, theoretical life or knowledge to God, or action to practical ends because Christianity momentarily allows for it.

The original understanding of time is a result of the coming together of paganism and Judaism, in other words the masculine and feminine in man. Borrowing from Orthodox Judaism to a certain extent, the Christian notion of time is a result of the mature form of time symbolized by the definitive abolition of the world's sin of which the millenarianism is one, possible guise. In the context of this essay, one such achievement is a result of the former, outright rejection of paganism or of the masculine, by way of its subsumption to the feminine that it had sought as its truth. Woman is the future of man. This assumption simultaneously replicates, modifies and displaces the classical, or Greek, problem of politics. This problem was defined as masculine as was that of the conservation of the conditions necessary for thought. In the feminine this problem was defined as the possibility of opening up oneself to otherness: Hobbes and his successors provide the fundamental configurations of a theory or a political science capable of serving one such end. If an opening is possible, it means that economics is shaping up as a definition of man's political identity: this suggests freeing economics from the early, masculine economic laws of the household that were primarily political in the Greek or pagan sense of the word. The "modern," political issue is that of the articulation between a reasoned politics, in the masculine sense of the term, and an open economy in the feminine sense of the term. This problem bridges the gap between politics and economy, or between economy and politics. The contemporary political imposition (symbolized by American politics) of an economy that is by construction apolitical or anti-political, and the various reactions (including those of extremists) that it implies, further complicates the myriad, contemporary political issues. These issues are evidenced by the sometimes frenzied, liberal "progressiveness" that is mostly feminine in its mature form as well as by the terrorist, identity reactions that are sometimes a reaction to the former. These reactions are carried out by a sentiment of plundering and of powerlessness that are mostly masculine. The "virilization" of contemporary, political battles is a result of the radicalization of the stakes that are unknowingly the most agitating for both of the human sexualities. The ultimate tension is reinforced as a result of man's rapport with time. Man is nostalgic, on the one hand, for a "natural" past that he idealizes as harmonious, while on the other hand being desirous of other, more innovative and open worlds. Far from acting merely on a global level of "globalization," this tension is felt at all levels, from the smallest to the largest and vice versa. It is at work on every individual just as it is on all peoples, cultures, States, and nations and organizes structures and propels the ensemble of our contemporary, political problems. This time is the effecter and the effect that we try to embrace because it is our time.

Notes

1 Plato, *Republic*, structure of book VIII.
2 Cf above, on the analogical relationship or, more precisely, fractal, from the largest to the smallest and reciprocally. Cf Plato, *Republic*, VIII and II (368d); cf Strauss L., *The City and Man*, chapter 2, pp. 143 et s.
3 Cf Plato, *Meno*'s issue, 81b–86c.
4 Cf the accusations aimed at Socrates regarding his meeting with Hippias (see Plato, *Apology of Socrates*, 32e–34a); cf Xenophon, *Les memorable*, IV, 4; cf the commentary proposed by Leo Strauss in *Xenophon's Socrates*, Cornell University Press, 1970, pp. 160–166, and p. 153; cf our commentary of the Straussian commentary of *The Memorable* in *Wisdom and the Feminine* (*La sagesse et le feminine*, l'Harmattan, 2005).
5 Cf above n. 8 of Chapter 3.
6 Cf Aristotle, *Nicomachean Ethics*, 1177b25–1178a5.
7 Likewise, 1178a20–25 and 1178b6–30.
8 Cf the outcome that the ultimate presence represents in Plato's *Symposium* of Diotima; cf Xenophon, *Symposium*, chapter VIII considering chapter II. Cf letters from 11 April to 28 May 1957 exchanged between Alexandre Kojève and Leo Strauss (Strauss L., *On Tyranny*, Gourevitch V. & Roth M. ed., The Free Press, 1991).

9   Cf Xenophon, *The Memorable*, III, 11 ; cf IV, 3 ; cf the author's comment cited here above on the Straussian commentary.
10 Plato, *Republic*, 592a–b.
11 Plato, *The Apology of Socrates*, 21b–23c.
12 Aristotle, *Politics*, 1253a 30–35.
13 Cf Strauss L., "On a Forgotten Art of Writing," *What Is Political Philosophy? And Other Studies*, chapter IX., The University of Chicago Press, Chicago.
14 In *The Thesmophories, Lysistrata*, and *The Assembly of Women*.
15 In the way in which "God" does so for the ensemble of his Creation, by naming them, man "dominates" nature both animals and plants—cf *Genesis*, 19–23; cf also 1, 1; cf *Jn* 1, 1.
16 Cf the meaning of the word "barbaric" in Greek, that designates those without language—lacking the capacity for rational thinking that shapes man, of which they are but faces.

Part III
Time

7
On Methodology

Abstract: *The subsumption of theory under practice that resulted from the Christian mix of Judaism and paganism makes room for a* future *oriented understanding of time. Time began, and it will end. Actually, post-humanist theorists have argued that time has* already ended. *They call it "the end of history." Such a statement frontally contradicts the feminine understanding of life. Theories may end, life never ends. Theories are always weaker than practice. Taking into account with utmost seriousness the theoretical possibility of an end of "history," this chapter shows why and to what extent such a theoretical approach to time is refuted* a priori *by the feminine practical approach of life.*

Keywords: *end of history, epistemology, Hegel, history, practice, theory*

Bibard, Laurent. *Sexuality and Globalization: An Introduction to a Phenomenology of Sexualities.* New York: Palgrave Macmillan, 2014. DOI: 10.1057/9781137469298.0014.

The dominance of the practical over the theoretical that is characteristic of our time distorts and exacerbates the nature of human sexualities thereby promoting a radicalization of their respective courses: on opposite ends of the spectrum are a masculine nihilism and a tendentiously repetitive call for equal rights. Man's contemporary struggle cannot be abridged to the abovementioned domination but rather implies a correlating transformation of the two sexual guises through which he is created. Whereas the guises' masculine side regrets its being, its feminine side seeks to be other than the way she senses herself now and as she has been from the beginning. Such binary constructs, with regard to both the past as well as anticipated futures, bring about an orthogonal intersection of, on the one hand, "ancient" and "modern" and, on the other, of action and thought. Untangling this knot requires shedding light on the meaning of time to each of the sexualities and to their potential associations. Examining the significance of infancy and maturity to both sexualities is essential to gain such clarity. Etymologically speaking, the term "infancy" refers to man's inability to speak either in political or ontological terms. Attempting to shed light on these states of being, emotions, and moods mean clarifying the meaning of language for each of the sexes. Analyzing the meaning of the words and language of which man is capable and which characterize him is indubitably requisite to understanding his relationship to time. The method for understanding this relationship is necessarily contained within language itself. Our line of questioning suggests that philosophy, like theology or any religious dogma seen from an outsider's perspective, is neither entirely philosophical nor un-philosophical. Our method does not rely on an unfolding, Hegelian dialectic meant to achieve its stages, its dynamics and the meaning of its concepts in a self-evident way. Neither is it a demonstration nor a monstration. It means liberating the space and time that, in the modern era, are held captive by the substantial burden of proof constituted by the prerogatives of economics, science and technology that shackle an otherwise unknowing man. The aim of this essay is anything but scientific as it suggests to and requires of the consenting reader to question his understanding of the world into which he was born. This world is characterized by a supreme liberation of the desire for perfection that, in turn, is sought out as a result of man's liberation from or desire for "nature" and "God" or gods. The contemporary era can be understood in terms of both a desire to control as well as that which contradicts or counteracts it. Total mastery of language would be symbolized by the writing of the *Books of Books* of Mallarmé's imagination. Man's ability to transform language into structured discourse, revealing the world in an exhaustive manner, is the ideal of a speech that would become *the* ultimate, supreme, unique, absolute and definitive word. The first tacit, then explicit claim of such an ideal was only possible starting with the European Renaissance. It was in Hegel's work, and even through his work, that the transition from the tacit to the explicit took place. Above all Hegel sought to encapsulate the history that in his eyes was primarily antagonistic to language and meaning—the terrifying space where emotions derail, where humans become agitated and where man, under siege by the interlacing of his desires and his fears, is silenced. Hegelian discourse allows for philosophical insights that wisely include, and therefore forgive, history's violence. By doing so he brings history to face its truth by unveiling its deeds and explaining its meaning. It is the discourse that absolutely identifies absolute difference: if difference cannot be defined as a movement toward the polar opposite of meaning, the identity that ensues from the identification of absolute alterity is but an illusion. The significance of this discourse, that recognizes liberty as the absolute, inherent difference with regard to the meaning that it encapsulates, recognizes liberty only to the extent that discourse itself is understood as an attempt to subjugate liberty to its own logic, to *the logic*. The ruminations of philosophy, opening one's mind to seeking the cruel truth of the world, are meaningless if the ultimate goal is not to arrest thought: being content with one's own wisdom or reinsuring the very world that one desires and seeks. What remains to be understood is the meaning of history as the divine accomplishment of man's freedom, achieved by way of a pact with nature's nature as well as its own nature, in the face of that which, at first glance, seems to be history's ostensible absurdity. Hegelian discourse essentially reunites all differences by acknowledging that they will also sooner or later distinguish themselves from one another.

Hegel is above all criticized for not abiding by the very genius of his claim that difference in the world must be recognized and defined comparatively and that all things achieve momentary distinctiveness when described and analyzed. The ambition of Hegelian logic, which is understood as representing the contrary to human individuality, assuming that it reveals humanity for what it is, either makes its case thereby eliminating individuality or fails in its effort thereby leading to its own undoing. He strives not to speak in absolutes, but rather to exist as the absolute by claiming to be the act by which the nothingness, absence, differentiation and absurdity of the world take part in the absolute. A part of this absolute is the fundamental decision to accept the reality of pervasive separation. Of that which exists, nothing precipitously eschews (in an often unforeseen manner) extinction or exists in a way that compromises the very meaning of being. That which exists is bound to the abysmal act of perishing. Sooner or later, however, and in a way that is recognizable only once it comes to be, the absolute coalesces as such, gaining self-consciousness as a movement toward identity on the basis of its difference. Sooner or later, even if only briefly, the absolute becomes the definitive identity of both the initial identity that defines it as well as the difference that it implacably becomes. The same can be said of discourse, as the unity or identity of meaning, its final objective being the "all other," in other words, history that itself is the realm of violence or absurdity of human life and the realm of non-discourse. The only way to understand discourse is to analyze it in relation to that which, at first, lies entirely outside of its realm. Outside the realm of theoretical discourse, which intends to reveal the world for what it is, is its opposite or action— history. The only difference between Shakespeare's words and Hegel's "story" (history) that discourse seeks to dominate is that the latter is not narrated by an idiot, but rather by a sage: "that which the world deems foolish in God is wiser than man's wisdom." Radical alterity is supposedly redeemed by a discourse that reaffirms itself, thereby paving the way for sage philosophy. Hegelian wisdom claims to be fundamentally "pagan" in Aristotelian terms, and as Hegel's quote at the end of the *Encyclopedia of Philosophical Sciences* suggests, wisdom is best achieved through contemplation. Hegelian wisdom, however, is initially of Christian inspiration before becoming modern: it sees at its foundation the ultimate power of will over meaning, or of the constant flux of categorizations into one another over static, categorical identity. Hegelian logic or dialectic is fundamentally modern because it is conceptualized as self-differentiation of itself. Classical logic or dialectic is above all defined as a quest for identity based on transcending difference that is eminently materialized by observable life itself. Yet Hegelian logic holds on the premise that it is driven to come full circle on itself—thereby guaranteeing an exhaustive and coherent reckoning. This logic, before being rationalized as the identity of identity *and of difference*, was the *identification* of identity and of difference, and sought to be masculine, or, in other words, the *identical* identity of identity and of difference. Hegelian discourse ultimately recognizes the differences in and by which the being defines itself only in order to align said differences toward their meaning or identification which alone is intended to give meaning to the notion of being. Whether Hegel realized it or not, his effort *excludes* difference from the self that it otherwise claims to recognize. In other words, the eminently masculine *decision* to move forward with aggregating discourse, the only way of ensuring meaningful discourse, is incomplete and biased—it excludes its contrary from its self. The contrary of one such decision or intention, absurd and therefore insignificant by construction, continuously resists the discursive affirmation of the aggregate discourse; time continues *after* Hegelian discourse, the claim that difference primes with regard to the identity of identity and of difference forcibly imposes its word even if, from a semantic standpoint, one such claim would be meaningless.

It is just as indicative of a certain truth that, on a practical level, the tenacious persistence of the claim that the identity of identity and of difference is illusory if not dangerous for mankind as is the reality that claims to encompass an aggregate discourse, namely history, as an absolute meaning. This affirmed reality, of no interest to its theoretically true character yet which is fundamentally practical for serving the reality that is significant in practice, is the very opposite of the truth sought out by the masculine discourse of philosophy, though modern it may be. The reality sought out by the discourse affirming the ultimate completeness and coherence of the world is the very identity sought out by the masculine in mankind. The multitude of trends or modern, "philosophical" works that to the contrary, claim—thereby becoming self-contradictory or remaining incomplete—the domination of difference over the identity of identity and difference constitute a primarily feminine approach to philosophy.

The feminine seeks to be difference because it is the alterity of self: in terms of discourse, its claim that difference predominates over identity is both contradictory and paradoxical. A discourse that seeks to be "philosophical" and is primarily feminine will ultimately, though in contradictory terms, claim, in the very terms of logical coherence and completeness, the unique reality that difference is the fundamental source of dynamism for all things. And yet incoherence or incompleteness matter less in this analysis than the reality that such discourse is indomitable. Such an affirmation bears witness to a more profound and fundamental reality: remaining free from any logical constraints in order to remain open to any and all otherness. Thus is the implicit affirmation that the process by which a discourse becomes whole and logical is not only irrelevant but also a threat to man's salvation. It is affirming, even if implicitly so, that man's happiness is dependent on something other than a reasoned discourse: man's word that claims to speak absolutely about the world in which he lives. For the feminine the practical realities of life count more than any theoretical discourse. Its reality, by way of the intractable diversity of its dynamics, avoids by construction all absolutes, be they discursive or practical. In its eminently masculine effort to identify the absolute that would create a world that is a comfortable home for man, philosophy knowingly leaves difference by the wayside because it assumes a preference for identity to difference. Doing so, however, means preferring the efficiency of action—even if it is meaningless—to the notion of truth. A philosophy that seeks to be even more complete must thus recognize the constituent contradiction that separates thought (ultimately spoken) from action (ultimately carried out) and vice versa. An aggregate philosophy will inevitably test its own limits or its own boundaries and is only complete when it fully recognizes the boundary that separates it from its other. Philosophy is only coherent and complete, in other words, in keeping with its initial intent, when it accepts the imposing feminine and its purviews: notably politics and religion. The present essay, meant to allow man to take his time, measures its success by being non-exclusively philosophical; it is intractably as such a practical, though unspoken decision, that might ultimately fail, and that seeks to be efficient. This decision is instrumental in unveiling realms for man's time, all of which have yet to be codified by modern habit. Because it is theoretical in nature, this essay cannot be excluded from philosophy's traces. It nevertheless remains on the fringe of modern-day voluntarism by which philosophy seeks to temper the domain of action under the identified and identifying yoke of meaning in the same way in which philosophical efforts ontologically and thematically structure the deafening battle between the masculine and the feminine. It is rather much closer to the soft, masculine approach by which Husserl attempted to "find" man's natural attitude (pre-scientific). It furthermore remains on the margins of a primarily feminine philosophy of difference, be it with a hermeneutic, linguistic or positivist logic outlook. However, since this essay is also by construction a practical exercise, and therefore "feminine," it would be unthinkable and absurd to try to recount the "whole" because "choosing and deciding" is paramount to the present exercise.

The purpose of this essay is therefore to propose a comprehensive vision of sensible decision-making in the context of an uncertain situation: "mindfulness" in action. Our purpose can only be described in this way to the degree that difference taps into our reflection on action and thought. The efforts made in this essay are therefore provisionally "Western" in nature. The notion of "Western" can be characterized as the delicate balance between thinking and doing which, itself, is the result of the desire to control. The West's other, at this point, is that which lies between thinking and doing, or perhaps that which lies between the identity of thought and the difference implied by action. It is possible to conceive thinking and doing as a single manifestation of the aggregate—redolent of ancient Chinese, and even ancient Indian thought and action. Placing itself between action and thought, the "West" is the East's other—the opposite of the assumption that thinking is doing and vice versa. It is not possible, when considering our time in aggregate terms, a time that is a result of globalization, to dismiss, or attempt to do so, the rapport between the typically Western approach to the difference between thinking and doing and the Eastern approach to the identity between thinking and doing. The way in which this identity is expressed and realized is, for the East that constructed it and that symbolizes it, the beneficial intertwining of writing, painting and speaking, or art, the understanding of the world and the decisions that ensue. Such an intertwining of painting, poetry and, in some cases, speaking, fulfills classical Chinese (Taoist) and Indian thought. Far from being valid for all of humanity Western assumptions follow, establish and fix a fundamental difference between "East" and "West." Once the path is determined, the direction in which globalization must be perceived (or fulfilled) becomes clear. Man's patent salvation can thus be identified as the effort to reconcile Western difference and Eastern identity. Identifying Western difference is accomplished by understanding the importance of ceasing the semantic classification of ideas that identify constant objects in the world (In turn these objects are expected to be constant otherwise no definition would be able to establish a stable meaning[1]).

The desire to render man capable of preserving a constant discourse about his constant world is an aspiration that is masculine in character: it is the result of the desire to maintain a reassuring discourse with regard to that which theoretically orients everything toward the absolute. This desire is eminently unilateral, at the very least, eminently theoretical. Feeling that one such desire is potentially lethal for the continued fluidity of things is feminine in nature. The discourse that seeks to be "uni-total" is by construct based on its disparity with that which it is not, or with practical discourse as such.² If masculine discourse consists of a rigorous aligning of categorical definitions that are co-dependent for meaning, its other implies at the very least the possibility of "hearing" the meaning of any unifying discourse, such as the expansion of the universe, "in other ways." It implies the discursively paradoxical possibility of not respecting categorical definitions. It implies seeking out and proposing a new language, following the example of the original Hegelian discourse and classifications, that is capable of newfound mobility without being trivial in everyday contexts. Although not unique in doing so, the Taoist tradition allows for the notable possibility of a discourse that is action-based and for action that is also discourse-based. The interaction between ideation and decision-making undermines the analytical difference between thought and action: thinking is deciding and vice versa. One such implicit proposition seeks to nullify the difference between the universal and the individual. In its immediate and unique reality, every action or gesture is thought at the same moment that it is seen and revealed, active mindfulness. This is our present aim. The immediacy of such thought and action, that are reciprocally constituent, implies the demanding labor or vigilant preparation to act (proactively) based on an attentive attending to the "entirety" of the world as it exists, in the moment it exists and in the place it exists for those who are in tune with it. Attaining absolute harmony between philosophy transformed into absolute knowledge and man is rare but, when it does happen, can be quite fecund. Our effort with regard to language is played out on this fine line: open or openness within the dynamic possibilities of language versus the possibility of fixing, misconstruing the meaning of our time. Preserving the semantic essence that our era forces upon conceptual terms implies acknowledging the desire to put into writing such a theory of semantics. It is moreover a refusal of the poetic expression of such meaning or, in the construct in which everything is linked and always susceptible to redefinition, the verbal expression of this same meaning. The static nature of modern language, as well as of its corresponding avatar, wide-ranging and directionless inventiveness, is a result of the objectifying endeavor that is, in turn, a result of the liberation of desire for mastery. Mastery means delimiting which, in turn, suggests defining, differentiating with specific meaning, or identifying the differences between the things of this world and those of others. Mastery implies playing the game of differentiation of everything without identifying the possibility of identifying everything. Mastery implies identifying while encapsulating the meaning of ideas, in other words identifying specifically that which is expected to express the essence of things. Hegelian logic, having distinguished itself on this point, significantly contributes to maintaining fluid categories: it remains that Hegelian logic seeks to close *all* discourse and does so by conferring upon difference or upon abstraction intended for understanding a semantic prerogative that is exceptionally determinant. Image should mean nothing to the Hegelian sage.[3] The active process that alternatively links and differentiates the image and the word whose written form is ventured is thus sunken into the night of contempt. Alternatively brought to light, an identity of identity and of difference, understood in the eminent context of our method, implies a continued ability to comprehend that whose decision begins by listening, or the reception of the absolute of life that is necessary for listening because it is its initial condition as well as its ultimate source.

Listening to what the East is, or was, before meeting the West, implies hearing the proximate movement by which hearing, thinking, and doing are accomplished simultaneously and without separation. Such an accomplishment is made possible by the process through which the masculine and feminine are in constant exchange. In Taoism, for example, this exchange is known as *yin* and *yang*. The gist of our proposal here is an attentively mediated dramatization between the "West" as it is described here and what the Toaists called the movement of the "ten thousand beings." Mediation brings to the forefront the process by which the expectations of the two sexes cross paths and foil one another. If the masculine is defined as desire or the spontaneous erection that stretches to meet the active affirmation of the identity it must create, the apex of its expression is the receptiveness of everything, peaceful openness to all that is given. If the feminine is the delimited identity of a space that is space for another, in a gesture that perpetually prepares its openness toward any "other" than itself, then the feminine's fundamental affirmation is the reassurance it finds in the obscure and impersonal persistence of life's paradoxical coming to be. The masculine's newfound identity in language—both discursive with regard to philosophy and legislative with regard to politics—joined with male virility, contributes to the spontaneous affirmation of its identity that is above all feminine. The creative availability of the feminine to all otherness, and especially the sexual, is seen as and represents the basis of the identity required by the masculine to try and find himself. The disjoined movement by which each of the sexualities is energized with the other in view, but still on its own terms, thereby establishing the differences, discrepancies and gaps that allow for these very dynamics, belong to all that exists and that which seeks to exist. If this intertwining ceases to be, so will life, or at the very least beings will cease to occur. The intertwining of the sexualities is the basis for all life regardless of one's sex. If it is thus necessary to try and identify the dynamic of each of the sexualities, to first anchor the vision on the apparent difference between men and women, it is within every man and every woman that the masculine and the feminine are at work thereby making life possible. We have also seen that the intertwining of these dynamics concerns the entirety of the world in which we live, on any scale. This intertwining is the fundamental process by which identities and differences, peaceful and warlike interactions between the same and the other, are created and disbanded. The entirety of the political system is, in this way, played out. This blending is also conditional upon the way in which the differences between the universal and the individual are identified and confounded, opening new realms, allowing for new arrangements, both in terms of action and in terms of thought. The three ways in which human sexuality plays itself out (logical difference, existential questions with regard to self and others, as well as the incomplete detachment of cultures on the basis of the "nature" of things) are now decipherable in a new way. It remains to be seen, in the following part, how the decision-making process unfolds.

Notes

1 Cf the meaning of the "Introduction psychologique du concept" by Kojève, A. in *Le Concept, le Temps, et le Discours,* Gallimard, 1990, p. 92 and s.
2 Cf Kojève A., *Essai d'une histoire raisonnée de la philosophie païenne,* t III; cf the preface of *L'athéisme* by the same author, Gallimard, 1998, p. 43, and p. 48 and s.
3 Cf Fessard G., *Hegel, le christianisme, et l'Histoire,* Part II, chapter III, compared to Part I, Excursus 1, 2, PUF, 1990.

8
Contradictions: Lives, Decisions, Thoughts

Abstract: *Approaching the feminine and the masculine on the basis of theory contradicts the feminine. A complete and coherent approach of genders must make room for a clear delimitation between theory and practice. It is thus necessarily a practical as well as a theoretical approach. Yet, it is reciprocally a theoretical approach as well as a practical one. This methodological necessity makes clear the vitalizing contradiction between feminine and masculine. This innate contradiction in fact represents the very place of humanity's rise. Misunderstanding each other and repairing their misunderstandings are the ways by which feminine and masculine ground the capacity of humans' humanization.*

Keywords: *conflict; contradiction; desire; dynamics; repairing; sexuality*

Bibard, Laurent. *Sexuality and Globalization: An Introduction to a Phenomenology of Sexualities.* New York: Palgrave Macmillan, 2014.
DOI: 10.1057/9781137469298.0015.

The identity that allows for an understanding of the meaning of life is not innate to the masculine. It therefore seeks, on the one hand, philosophy's identifying discourse that will lead it to wisdom, and on the other hand, political legislation, preferably in written laws. The feminine seeks openness, poetry, the arts and the mystery of the gods because the feminine is not born with the innate difference from which meaning originates. Inhabiting man from birth is the surprise that the world, which so suddenly comes to his attention reveals its hidden face; the feminine is the space in which life is renewed from generation to generation. The feminine is inherently the law or the commandment that the masculine speaks; whereas the masculine symbolizes the other sought out by the feminine. The beginning, or childhood, of each of the sexualities represents the adult form of its other. From the sexes, products of a temporal interlacing of the vectored processes, emerges a field of thought for many misunderstandings, psychologically speaking, that psychoanalysis, followed by its partisan disciplines attempt with some success to identify, characterize, and sometimes unravel. Such fields of thought are also applicable on the largest scale: from paganisms to Judaism the masculine seeks "Mother Nature" while the feminine is ultimately reaching out to "God the Father." Maturation for each of the sexes implies the realization for each that it is or "exists as" the spontaneous, or uncalculated, movement toward the other. In other words a movement that is neither conscious nor voluntarily chosen. This tension means that each sex sees the shape of the other as a possible image of salvation—at the very least, satisfying the desire that constitutes each sex. The movement of each sex is desire itself as a vectored tension, fueled by the creation of the image of the other that it seeks. This image is not necessarily objectal; it is, however, intractably at least partially projective, insofar as it is coenesthesically, kinesthetically and perceptively fueled and created. For each of the sexes, "existing" means reaching out incessantly toward the other who is by definition absence; an "other" or alterity (as it turns out, in the case of the masculine, the "same") incessantly recomposed, as a result of life-defining events; the innate memory that allows such a being to be real; and the interlacing of both. These interlacings are further complicated by the individual interlacings that constitute every human born from the heterogenesis that until now defined it. Man's defining task is, in other words, elucidating and verbalizing that which is possible, the active memory that allows every individual to live, thereby thinking and deciding to live, reflecting upon and determining his life. Failing to execute this task results metaphorically and sooner or later literally in his early demise. For man standing tall and being fully human is tantamount to using both his capacity to remember and to forget, to be present and to project, as well as his ability to be either in motion or immobile not to mention the choice of being responsible or not. Modernity reinforces, bends and exacerbates the tension between two such possibilities—some think about living, others about dying. It is so because the desire for perfection, for mastery or for control is limitless and unforgiving: the incessant demand that the finest work be achieved. In the eyes of each sex, the best is the other that it now seeks to be. The greatest danger resides, however, in the exclusion of each sex by the other, when each alone wants to fulfill its happiness and its luck. Women therefore put forth their identity and make soldiers of themselves while allocating resources to creation and action whereas men put forth their unique difference and take pleasure in the fundamental, nihilistic ontological worthlessness while pathologically exacerbating their identity of stationary politics. The vitality of it all is only guaranteed in proportion to the theoretical or practical, conscious or unconscious, recognition that each sex is indeed the means by which the other creates an image of itself. Otherwise the respective energies are torn apart without enriching one another—and the desert grows.

A unilateral and single time vector that is trending toward a future perspective can characterize the aforementioned modernity. Evident in this line of thinking is the virilization of each of the sexes that results in a conscious or unconscious solipsistic exacerbation of its natural dynamic. The being that is the source of all things is therefore, in one way or another, considered unworthy if not bad: that which is good and worthy is reserved for man's future. This holds true for each sex: that which is good is in each one's future, the masculine for the feminine and the feminine for the masculine provided that the masculine and the feminine are not sought out for the ways in which each fulfills its own dynamic but rather *in order to satisfy* the feminine and the masculine. In other words each is perceived as it is preyed upon by its other. The feminine form feeds the masculine's desire for meaning and yet is relegated to fulfilling his sexual desires only; the masculine strength clearly serves to protect the community—a community that is strictly defined and structured according to the feminine. The use value thus dominates, reigning over all aspects of life.

The dominant "modernity" diverges from the former world that was masculine in character: well-defined hierarchy, clearly defined practical norms, thought to be eternal and seeking to be as stable as possible. On a political level it was fundamentally collective in nature and defined in terms of a past that was a blueprint for a given future and therefore of the present. Motion is to rest as modernity is to the ancient world. In the same way that politics was the dominant structure of the ancient world, economics and its corollary, law reign in the contemporary world. The contemporary political issue is one of articulating domination by one or by the others. In a fundamental way this problem is borne from the opposition of progressive and conservative politics if not from anarchy and totalitarianism. The tension at hand is not, however, one that opposes the terms masculine and feminine any more than it opposes "modern" masculine and feminine with their "ancient" equivalents. Modernity presents a virile feminine that reactively opposes an equally virile, yet unstable masculine. In a general sense the modern affirmation of mastery and/or control is evidence of human existence: the living human is above all, in one way or another raised in a community and vectors himself inward as an autonomous element progressively isolated from the community. In this respect he takes on a primarily feminine role: an initially collective identity that tends toward difference by which and as which all *individuals* affirm their identity as an outer reflection of their community. The tendency for man to move away from his collective past toward a future of individuality is the very essence of his being. The initially masculine movement by which man, discovering himself as a dislodged being, finds direction by seeking the absolute is thus secondary. Secondary and quite likely fundamental to the humanity of human beings: as a result of the latter movement the initial one seemingly liberates man from nature and perhaps even his gods. He is otherwise a disruption and an ecological menace. It is, in other words, critical to living humans that the *collective* nature of life trump individualism. From the moment that natural individualization in and for which the feminine finds source is given credence by the primarily masculine search for the absolute and his condition that is man's natural maladjustment to nature, individuation becomes man's route to liberation from nature and potentially even from his gods. He is not simply destruction of the community that assures the continuation of life.

In the end, the natural vectoring of man as a function of time can be structured in the following way:

Past	Future
Community	Individuality
Identity	Difference
Practical silence	Theoretical discourse
Natural state of man	Stated goals
Unconsciously active	Self-awareness, autonomy
Spontaneity	Imagined state of limitless
Empirical and fundamentally	and timeless space bounded reality

As a reaction to his natural state, the masculine vectoring of man as a function of the space that he seeks for himself takes on the following characteristics:

Present	Future
Individuality	World
Difference	Identity
Doubt, possibility of discourse	Truth
Self-awareness as projected	Life Theoretical (Greek) absence

* * *

"Ancient" and "masculine" on the one hand and "modern" and "feminine" on the other are analogous only to an extent. Following this logic, paganism and Judaism are masculine and feminine respectively in a masculine context whereas, for example, secular Christianity and Islam are feminine and masculine respectively in a feminine context. The latter hypothesis should be taken with considerable reservation: the possibility of a formally recursive use of the terms "masculine" and "feminine" does not allow for a direct application of its meaning: such a semantic back-and-forth could only take on meaning in a scientific (modern) context of an applied *sociology* of said categories. In other words depending on an *empirical* test of theories that have to be methodologically tested. Determinant for man is nevertheless the active contradiction by which youth, infancy, or the origin of each of the sexes contains, at least in the imagined terms of desire, the "adult" or achieved meaning of the other. That which each of the sexualities seeks from the other is what the other seeks to escape in itself: the future of each is the past of the other. Strictly submitting itself to the desire of the other is tantamount, for each sex, to reducing itself to the rank of a futureless infancy, a fundamentally contradictory infancy with a radically pejorative outlook. It is nevertheless this very danger, though, that enables man to conceive time in such a way.

Whether, in scientific or modern terms it can be affirmed that man erects himself, from the foundation of his animalistic nature and, as a result of the fertile, for contradictory weaving of the sexes, or that it is sufficient, in "ancient" terms, to note the educational value of the repeatedly played out ontogeny, the following becomes clear.

Human gender dynamics are fundamentally contradictory. The very first evidence of this contradictory constitution can be found in the erratic behavior typical of the masculine compared with the identity stretching out toward itself by which the feminine always first experiences itself and by which the living being is both reproduction and survival: ousted from this very space, inhabited by disbelief, questioning and doubt, the masculine represents sooner or later a threat to the survival of his community. If it is important to provide man with a fertile mythology about his phylogenesis, let us suppose[1] that man's erectile ability, together with his ability to use an opposable thumb for gripping, helps differentiate him from the animal that he used to be and that is a result of the eminently human possibility that the female[2] refuses to engage in a sexual act. It is therefore dual disinclinations that give way to the two mediations by which man finds his complete and fulfilled humanity. At the individual level ontogeny operates analogically with phylogenesis: the dual movement that is constituted by the forbidding of incest on the one hand and on the other the education that will sooner or later become a contradiction to a child's natural impulse, bring to life, in terms of education, the two primary mediations that allow for man to face the test of his split personality and the consciousness that results from it that is, sooner or later, *self-consciousness*. This schism occurs between spontaneity and restraint on the one side and between the self and the other sex on the other side. This dual schism is a result of the single movement through which an individual identifies as such within its community: learning alterity means learning to restrain spontaneity. Sexual alterity is the fundamental one: a genesis for experiencing, feeling, discerning, identifying and smoothing out one by one its other forms. It is a result of the fundamental character of *inhibited* desire that will define man and through which he will be defined: my future is my other, my other is the other sex as my reality, symbol and fantasy; in and as the very act of desiring it in the manner in which I construct it, I unknowingly transgress what it wants from and for itself. Sooner or later I instigate a refusal on its part, a reticence to show itself as I want it, to subscribe to the model of desire that I am and that I have. So long as nothing comes between us, I learn nothing, but rather live. A new realm of questioning, doubt, interrogation, violence, refusal, and creativity resulting in the genesis of human culture opens as soon as the other sex intervenes between my desire and the satisfaction of my desire. This human is the contradictory weaving of the sexual dynamics that are its dual pillars. This very weaving results in the opening of a space and of time that are proper to man. These concepts are in fact the very definition of man as a creative manifestation. The dual action that results in my becoming man is the non-conformity of my sexual other to my desire and the non-conformity of what I myself am, compared to its expectations, that may become apparent to me. By identifying myself in this way, compared to that which I now see as my other, I become self-conscious because of what and who I am not. Doing so I realize through my other that I may encounter an obstruction to the fulfillment of my desire. This obstruction is ultimately the lull in the dynamic that allows me to reach out toward myself as an accomplishment, now composed of my other sexuality. At first spontaneously oriented toward my future, I am thus impeded from attaining it or from constructing myself. I am a prisoner in the present shackled to a past which will not serve my ambitions for reaching a future. The primary reason for the shackles in which I am trapped is the contradictory desire of my archetypal other sex. My consciousness of self as a past time vectored toward the future is suddenly aroused—in the original meaning of the term—by the fundamentally contradictory desire for the sex that is not mine. Man's time is the desire for and of the other.

And yet man is never just man (male) or woman (female), for he is never just masculine nor feminine. The raw heterogenesis from which he is born (until the next possible techno-scientific order takes place), means that he is in essence both masculine and feminine and feminine and masculine, in variable proportions that do not correlate with his recognizable anatomical sex. In other words the proportion is determined on an individual level, depending on the events that define his life, especially where these occur during his prime infancy, the way in which the constitutive and contradictory dynamic by which man becomes self-conscious as time. To and within each human being the desire is at work in both the accusative and in the dative, the desire that makes me my own time: man's time is the desire for and of the other.

* * *

Being the very time that is the contradictory vectorization of my arrival at self-consciousness means that I am the other individual, divisible into two sexualities that are equally alive and for which I am the ultimate proof of their problematic encounter. In other words, I am multiple from the beginning at which time I wanted to be one, when I would have liked to be one. For man, wanting to be "one" is paramount to being autonomous, to being the sovereign author of his world, the captain of his life, who controls its conditions and deadlines, much like he is when faced with controlled fortune. Man's archetypal fortune is being born as two. As a "modern" being I dream of minimizing this boiling river of pain and contradictions without realizing that the very melting pot of tension nourishes me, either man or woman, and my fertility. As an "ancient" being I see my own schism and for this reason my life. I organize the actions necessary for carrying out life according to a primordial receptivity with regard to that which surrounds me in the world—in nature, in God or in "gods." Modernity's constitutive, driving force is the elimination of sexual difference. The normative base upon which the "ancient" masculine is erected is the sexual schism that is duly stratified in a hierarchy.

Even if his community is composed of yet-to-be humanized, living beings man is indomitably vectored toward a self-autonomous nature based on the assumption of his prior, archaic appartenance to his (or her) community. Understood according to this onto-anthropogenetic or phylo-anthropogenetic assumption, "modernity" as we have seen and described it is necessary or "natural." It is the indomitable adolescence of living man. Such an observation nevertheless presupposes an acknowledgment of man as *two*, that is to say bi-sexual. Accepting his bi-sexuality is an eminently "classic" or ancient way of thinking and is a primarily masculine approach vectored not toward individuality but rather toward the natural vision of man. The ancient's approach, seen as conventional by modern man, is fundamental to perceiving the natural character of modernity.[3] Similarly, only a modern, intellectual culture allows man to clearly understand the "natural" state of sexuality: the instant at which sexuality loses its obviousness is the moment at which its fundamental dynamics reveal themselves. No matter which sex one is, man is sooner or later an "adolescent," in other words he rebuffs his origins by insisting that he be *one*; this very rebuffing means that, as a mature adult he recognizes the indomitable duality of the sexes. This indomitability is not a result of an immobile and unchangeable juxtaposition, but rather the result of an indefinitely replayed game of intricate yet fertile differences. Because of these intricate situations and by virtue of its provisional tension man's adolescence seeks to eliminate these differences. Ancient Taoism reveals how and by which dynamics these intricacies, while preparing for death at the time of conception, also make way for the life of a newborn.[4] Man's life consists of demystifying these intricacies to the best of his ability thereby affirming his status as a living being all while condemning him to death. Before undertaking such an effort man is not human per se but rather a speechless child, a simple and spontaneous rhapsody of the vital, divine momentum that is his origin. Beyond these attempts he is either divine or he is no longer alive. Existing as a living human is tantamount to (a) unraveling the aggregate that creates and tries to impede life—a happy life, man's good life— and (b) *being* this very effort. A life whose path has been laid, chosen willingly and conscientiously is always foremost recognition of the ambiguous tension by which man desires and seeks to annihilate himself. Man ontologically refuses to allow life to be simply "good" or "happy." Doing so creates considerable tension between thinking and doing, knowing and wanting, because thinking or knowing could potentially stifle desire: an overly-heightened self-consciousness suffocates self-consciousness because it compromises the fundamental conditions necessary for vital consciousness of existing in a given situation.[5]

Rounding out our original analysis implied contextualizing the notion of "decision-making." Such contextualization implies an understanding of time for which we outlined the beginning and unveiled the primary space in which it emerges. This space consists of the fertile ground that separates man's dual sexualities. We went on to demonstrate that "modernity" consists, in particular, of obliterating this separation for the benefit of the asexualized notion of virility—which is both masculine and feminine. The propensity for "modernity," obliterating the bi-sexuality of humans, is not entirely effective. The contemporary dynamic that defines the way in which sexuality must be treated on an intellectual plane strengthens the tension between "ancient" bi-sexuality and "modern" de-sexualization of man. Time was earlier understood to be the contradictory, constitutive tension (therefore always both fertile and morbid) between the two sexes that are understood as the feminine dynamic of the identical toward difference, and the masculine dynamic of difference toward identical. In a feminine world, "modernity" implies the obliteration of the difference in the sexes and therefore of time. Obliterating time in such a way is, in the end, tantamount to doing so to man who is the corporeal dynamism that is catalyzed by his natural and constitutive sexual contradiction.

It remains to be seen, in order to conclude our analysis by analyzing time itself, how the tension between modernity and the ancient world plays out.

Notes

1. In conformity with the epistemological status of modern science this will forever retain its status of hypothesis.
2. Cf our *La Sagesse et le féminin,* Part II, last section.
3. Cf the intention of Tocqueville's work, notably *Democracy in America,* Vol. 2, Part IV, chapters VI, VII & VIII.
4. Cf Eyssalet J.M. *Le secret de la maison des ancêtres*, Editions de la Maisnie, 1990, p. 214 and following and p. 449 and following.
5. A philosophical compromise to which Nietzche was particularly sensitive.

9
Love as a Responsible Presence

Abstract: *Taking into account the previous methodological warnings, this chapter presents a new understanding of the notion of presence. Presence results from a positive interlacing of feminine and masculine. Such a positive interlacing concerns individuals as well as civilizations: the chapter makes clear the extent to which, independently of her/his apparent anatomy, each individual is always at once feminine and masculine and reciprocally. Such a clarification orients the reader toward capturing what is essential in the ancient Chinese Taoism teaching. The current globalization dynamic is consequently to be revisited on the basis of the previous chapters.*

Keywords: *action; contemplation; decision-making; love; presence; responsibility*

Bibard, Laurent. *Sexuality and Globalization: An Introduction to a Phenomenology of Sexualities.* New York: Palgrave Macmillan, 2014. DOI: 10.1057/9781137469298.0016.

By rendering possible the secular subsumption of pagan "nature" to the all-powerful divine, Christianity implicitly vectors man's time according to the eminently theological notion of parousia. Though located within the necessary eternity of its own coming, oriented from the past toward the future, the paradoxical time of Christ is a synonym for the very moment of the singular event that constitutes his incarnation, his death and his resurrection. It is ordained that man always be his incarnation, death and resurrection. Each instant that is piously lived follows the dynamic in which profane time is, according to this model, understood. At birth man suffers from the obligation to absolve his sins or to strive incessantly to perfect nature, both human and non-human, by way of his work.[1] This effort fundamentally defines man as an act of time reaching toward the realization of his good while necessarily accepting the posit that he is imperfect at birth. Man's "modernity" is his ability to respect the original blueprint of the masculine. Whereas ancient times were that of the masculine's maturity or of its achievement to the detriment of the feminine that, too, was held to its own original blueprint, modern times are that of the masculine's remaining in its aurora or in the infancy of its dynamic. Man's remaining in this space correlates to the feminine's achievement, to its maturity. Our starting point, observing the scarcity of time, is primarily masculine. Feminism justly and precisely recognizes that the feminine has until now been refused its place, public recognition and space. Lacking public space for the feminine is tantamount to lacking the time that allows it to self-accomplish, whereas lacking time to mature, for the masculine, is tantamount to lacking the space or the place he seeks for himself in the world. If each of the sexes were to constrain its other in such a way, the liberation of the feminine that is at least partially a result of its former captivity in its own infancy or in the absence of language by the masculine bends the masculine's time toward the future, all while provoking modern "self-consciousness." Self-consciousness replaces the so-called ancient "virtue" that was a function of "nature." This viril reversal inserts into both heart and spirit the idea that the future, necessarily better than the past, can be decided consciously and voluntarily as opposed to a past that had already been survived. This unilateral projection of time toward the future unconsciously establishes man in a way that makes his past seem rash. The past, from which a fresh start must be made, should not be sensible to the "modern" man. This is observable within the context of contemporary, everyday life. More specifically the elders and the dead are only understood as a result of a supposedly eternal "youth" of the former. One must always be young or risk being nothing. Making a show of power is incontrovertible for heightened vigor and the grandest performances (true no matter the domain in question) without which man is momentarily marginalized. The aggregate of these requirements is continually ordained under the assumption that the transparency and control, or mastery, encountered in the beginning of our analysis reign. In terms of both knowledge (transparency) and action (control), this assumption implies yet another according to which man is perfectly self-conscious, or at least free from any possible unconscious acting in his place. This hypothesis is not "realistic" and therefore not reasonable for the simple reason that man's origin structures and conditions him despite the fact that today he is characterized by the contemporary effort at returning to himself in the hopes of gaining absolute control over himself as a living being.

The viril reactions, primarily masculine, that seek to return to past realities of former, ancient worlds, overlooking the conditions of this world, are no longer pertinent or viable: commencing the present from a clean slate, to the benefit of the past and against the original dominance accorded to the future, represents a dangerous step backward. The occasional attempt to transmit pagan moderation is of the upmost importance in this context. This effort can resemble man's openness to the three "ekstases" of time that allow him to become man. His openness first requires that he recognize man's active and imperative modern vectoring toward himself as perfection, perfecting action, mastery and knowledge that will sooner or later become practical. This perfection further requires that man attempt to meditate to what extent control and mastery are pertinent: masculine or feminine, feminine or masculine, man never masters nor controls beyond the basis of having one day been born into or expelled into this world. No matter how he sees himself, his desire for control is inevitably founded on the impersonal basis of the source of his own life that always allows him to experience himself, though sometimes unknowingly so, and that sometimes allows him to discover himself. No matter how invigorating the intensity with which he imagines his future, man's foundation for accomplishing his projects is in the past that he is. In reality his true presence is the very game between his desires and his fears, between his dreams and his archaic yet persistent origins. Whereas the principle of pleasure moves him toward his future, the principle of reality holds him back in the web of the past. The less he imitates what he already was, the more the uncertainty toward which he projects himself feeds his fears and his shortcomings like the opening of the possibilities of which he dreams. The more he wishes to open himself to the unknown that sooner or later takes the shape of salvation,[2] the more he risks, unknowingly, persisting in reproducing what he already knows how to do. In other words, the more that man believes that he is embarking in a new future, the more he risks regressing into his archaic form. Risking such a regression is not a guarantee that it will happen. It means that the future of which he dreams is, in its anticipated form, still misleading: assuming that the anticipated form is promising, it guarantees neither the effort of its acts nor the effects of the effort dedicated to making it a reality: he who tries to act the angel risks acting the brute. Nothing that seeks to be angelic, that drags man back down unknowingly into his archaisms, can protect man from himself. To the contrary, it is in the definition of his goals, as well as in the effort to make them pertinent to the present, that man's true repos lies, his position of self as a whole man. Man's "repos" in this context signifies a constant renewal of self based on the present which we must recognize before acting upon it. Our efforts up to this point have prepared us for this conclusion that man's present is the point of view that he incarnates—a point of view that he must accept, or at least recognize wholly, by accomplishing his destiny. The achievement of man's destiny begins paradoxically with his explicit attempt to listen, to remain open to the entirety of that which the world, or worlds, into which he is born may offer him. None of man's behavior is authentic if not a result of the prerequisite effort to remain open to what the future may hold regardless of its dynamism. And yet that which man can expect is above all himself as he is presented as a memory of his fundamental makeup. This memory is innate and immediately acquired first by birthright then by way of the adventures that mark his life. Even his desires are a result firstly of the memory that he *is,* and that he later *has,* through good times and bad, by taking part in the world that surrounds him and that contributes to forming his stature and makeup. The only term that man must respect is his present which can be described as dynamic: contradictorily composed of the fertile and dangerous intertwining of the sexes that form and tie him together. Man's present is his decision. It courageously and fundamentally reunites his "ekstasies" that, time after time opposed, are his past and future, his desires, his memories, his fears and his dreams. Without the living contradictions that are masculine and feminine, no space would exist in allowing man the possibility of gaining enough distance from himself as a living being. Humanity is merely this very possibility of man's presence—not the immediately contemplative presence, as paganism would have it, but rather an imminently responsible presence. The risk at hand is that of an abysmal failure, but despite this risk humanity is the audacity to speak, act or seek meaning in the world. In the masculine or pagan sense of the word, presence ignores its other, the "do" momentum by which the feminine hastens its truth. The truth of both man's masculine and feminine truths is in the eminently responsible decision to accept, in the present, that which, in this world, including oneself, is unavoidable in deciding what must be accomplished. Under one such guise man is incapable of guaranteeing the *outcome* of his efforts—but he must put forth his best *effort* regardless of the outcome. Integral to this obligation is the requirement of expecting nothing from the start and, no matter the circumstances nor the problem that motivates him, to allow himself to understand the circumstances and then to mature as a result.

This describes, in the masculine context, the responsible, decision-making process that he tries to be. The feminine side of this process is self-evident in the same way as, in the Japanese tradition, the act of trying to hit a target with an arrow without looking at the target. One such letting go with regard to desire and fear presupposes itself: learning to let go in order to achieve a goal implies knowing how to let go in order to try. The evident, logical impossibility that is imposed lends credibility to the ancients and their silence. Here, merely *saying* becomes a self-contradiction. It only makes sense to try to *do* something. This is the frame of all discourse including practical discourse especially insofar as this essay is concerned.

* * *

The written traditions have usually been particularly conservative considering the means it has provided itself to ensure its passage from generation to generation. The vast majority of traditions that man has invented are oral ones. Writing is particularly useful in elaborating the laws that govern a community and in providing man's masculine stability in the earthly world. Thus the written word alternately takes the form of codified law, theoretical constructs, religious revelations, or of a variety of mysterious stories of varied meaning. On the other hand storytelling is giving the word the strength of its infancy, where it begins, by inaugurating man's movement from silence to language. He may thus differentiate between the reasoned and the absurd. Neither philosophy nor the sacred texts is the achievement of man's wisdom: philosophy's fault is its self-avowed obsession with that which it is missing, and the sacred texts are but the trace of that to which they attempt to orient man. If man's wisdom is discursive, his wisdom is biased because it is incomplete. It is founded within the very decision to be *only* a discourse and excludes the ultimate silence upon which, whether it wants to or not, it gains traction. A complete *discourse* realizes sooner or later that, as such, the very human decision not to say but to do or to listen remains outside of its construct. Writing or listening to a poem, a work of art, praying, creating a tool: our current discourse whose value is dependent upon its imminent completion, has reveled a few, fundamental differences between what we decided to call the masculine and the feminine of man. Exposing these differences allowed for a brief appearance of man as this energizing difference given the contradictory fertility of his potential conflicts. Man is in fact an individual just as the totality of past and future worlds, the Orientals and the Westerners, the polytheists and the monotheists, the believers or the atheists. What has proven to be important for the world in which the author of this essay, without his prior consent, belongs is the radicalization of the difference between the feminine and the masculine that are symbolized by the two, sovereign civilizations of paganism and Judaism. This radicalization later allowed, in favor of liberating the too-human desire to survive, for a notable, if not violent exacerbation. What we proposed here, in line with that which ancient Taoism silently teaches, is principally motivated by the malaise of our civilization that covers the globe under the guise of what we now call "globalization." The purpose of this essay was to stimulate thought in the direction of a notion that is universally imposed as a nodal theme of our time: the complicated and intricate encounter of the sexes. Man's fate, on both an individual and an aggregate level, is dependent upon this encounter. In the most demanding meaning of the verb "to make," making love has become the most urgent of acts in man's quest to remain happily dignified of his name. It is also the most difficult of acts that requires remaining in the human present as the present itself—to offer oneself a "present."

Such a deed implies endeavoring, listening to our time and making ourselves its servant or its silent receptacle, relearning how to best take our time. Doing so is every man and woman's eminent human responsibility.

Notes

1. Cf Strauss L., *Natural Right and History*, chapter V, b.
2. Obviously including for man's masculine for which the unknown is then the basis that he is not innately for himself.

Bibliography

Aristophanes (2006). *The Complete Plays of Aristophanes*, Bantam Classic, New York.
Aristotle (2009). *The Nicomachean Ethics*, Oxford University Press, New York.
Aristotle (1998). *The Metaphysics*, Penguin Classics, Penguin Books, London.
Aristotle (1995). *Politics*, Oxford University Press, New York.
Bibard, L. (2005). *La Sagesse et le féminin*, L'Harmattan, Paris.
Bourgeois B. (1992). "La déraison historique", in *Etudes hégéliennes, Raison et décision*, PUF, Paris.
Buber, M. (1967). *On Judaism*, Shoken Books, New York.
Descartes, R. (2005). *Discourse on the Method of Rightly Conducting the Reason, and Seeking Truth in the Sciences*. 1st World Library—Literary Society, UK.
Descartes, R. (2003). *Meditations and Other Metaphysical Writings*, Penguin Classics, Penguin Books, London.
Eyssalet, J.M. (1990). *Le secret de la maison des ancêtres*, Editions de la Maisnie, Paris.
Fessard, G. (1990). *Hegel, le christianisme, et l'Histoire*, PUF, Paris.
The Holy Bible (1999). King James Version, American Bible Society, New York.
Hegel, W.G.F. (2007). *Lectures on the Philosophy of Religion*, Oxford University Press, New York.
Hobbes, T. (1968). *Leviathan*, Penguin Classics, Penguin Books, London.

Kojève, A. (1964). "L'origine chrétienne des sciences modernes", in *Mélanges Alexandre Koyré II*, Paris.
Kojève, A. (1990). "Introduction Psychologique Du Concept" by Kojève, A. in *Le Concept, le Temps, et le Discours*, Gallimard, Paris.
Kojève, A. (1972). *Essai d'une histoire raisonnée de la philosophie païenne*, t III, Gallimard, Paris.
Kojève, A. (1998). *L'athéisme*, Gallimard, Paris.
Locke, J. (1980). *Second Treatise of Government*, Hackett Publishing Company, Indianapolis and Cambridge.
Machiavelli, N. (1998). *The Prince*, The University of Chicago Press, Chicago.
Montesquieu, C. de, Baron de Segondat (1949). *The Spirit of the Laws*, MacMillan, New York.
Plato (2005). *Protagoras and Meno*, Penguin Classics, Penguin Books, London.
Plato (2002). *Five Dialogues: Euthyphro, Apology, Crito, Meno, Phaedo*, Hackett Publishing Company Inc.
Plato (1999). *The Symposium*, Penguin Classics, Penguin Books, London.
Plato (1968). *The Republic*, Library of Congress.
Stewart, I. (2002). *Does God Play Dice? The New Mathematics of Chaos*, Blackwell Publishing.
Strauss, L. (1991). *On Tyranny*, The Free Press, Glencoe.
Strauss, L. (1975). "The Three Waves of Modernity", in *Political Philosophy, Six Essays by Leo Strauss*, Pegasus, Indianapolis and New York.
Strauss, L. (1970). *Xenophon's Socrates*, Cornell University Press, Cornell.
Strauss, L. (1964). *The City and Man*, University of Chicago Press, Chicago.
Strauss, L. (1959). *What is Political Philosophy ? And other Studies*, The University of Chicago Press, Chicago.
Strauss, L. (1958). *Thoughts on Machiavelli*, University of Washington Press, Washington.
Strauss, L. (1953). *Natural Right and History*, University of Chicago Press, Chicago.
Tocqueville, A. de. (2003). *Democracy in America*, Penguin Classics, Penguin Books, London.
Xenophon (2001). *Memorabilia*, Cornell University Press, Cornell.

Index

absolute, 8, 29, 60, 73–4
action, 33–4, 75, 91
advertising, 40
alterity, 48–56, 71–3, 80, 84
anarchism, 61
ancient, 3, 32–4, 70, 75, 82, 83, 84, 91
anthropology, 20, 27
Aristophanes, 62
Aristotle, 17, 27, 60
artisans, 13
arts, 80
attitude, 21, 28, 32, 74

biotechnology, 3
birth, 15–16, 50, 59–60, 80
bi-sexuality, 44, 86, 87
body, 60–1
belief, 23, 62

certainty, 8, 47–51, 53–6, 63, 64
chiasmus, 52–6
childhood, 42, 80
Chinese thought, 75
Christianity, 20, 21, 32, 57, 90
  Crucifixion, 26–9
  development of, 26–9
  roots of, 21–5, 29
  science and, 28
  secularization of, 20, 28–9, 32, 33, 34, 83, 90
  time and, 65
classic, 32, 62, 65, 72, 75, 86
coherence/coherent, 25, 63, 73
collectivism, 82

commandments, 23, 25, 31, 62, 80
community, 7, 11, 23, 48, 53, 55, 61, 63, 64, 81
completeness, 73
complexity, 8–9
consciousness, 2, 84–6
conservatives, 82
contemplation, 21, 27, 72, 89
contradiction, 31, 33, 44, 74, 79, 83–4, 86, 88, 92
control, *see* mastery
convention, 58
culture, 45, 58, 81

death
  avoidance of, 35
  fear of, 12, 29
  transcending, 26
decision-making, 8, 74–8, 87–8
Descartes, Rene, 10, 12–16, 18–20, 28, 29
desire, 33–4, 35, 53, 63, 80, 84–6
dialectics, 70, 72
difference/differenciation, 32, 37–8, 40–4, 48–56, 64, 65, 71–8, 80–8, 94
discourse, 45, 71–6, 80, 94
Discourse on Method
  (Descartes), 12–14
Divine power, 22, 27
dual sexualities, 44, 77–8

East, 75, 77
economy, 3, 6–9, 11–13, 29–30, 65
education, 7, 35, 59, 84
ekstases, 91, 92
employment, 7–8
epistemology, 12, 69
equilibrium, 58, 59
eternity, 24, 51, 54, 55, 58, 90
Europe, 12, 17, 19, 20, 22, 29, 30, 32, 71
evidence, 2, 11, 49, 54, 61, 62, 66, 82, 84
existence/existential, 7–9, 11, 13, 15, 17–19, 23, 29, 31, 37, 40–1, 47–51, 59–63, 78, 82
Eyssalet, Jean-Marc, 88

faith, 62
fear, 8, 9, 11, 12, 29, 33–5
feminine, 3, 15–16, 34, 37–40, 52–7, 61, 64, 70, 73, 77, 80–3, 90
feminine identity, 47–50, 53, 81
feminism, 39, 42–3, 62
fertility, 15–16, 47, 86
fortune, 15–16, 18, 30–1
fractal morals, 39–45
freedom, 55, 71

gender dynamics, 84–6
genetics, 3
global economy, 6–9
globalization, 2–3, 31–4, 66, 89, 94
    concept of, 3
    psychology and, 41–2
    sexuality and, 2–3, 41
    time and, 75
God, 22–4, 26–8, 32, 58, 60, 62–4, 80, 86
government, 61
Greek gods, 24, 25
Greek philosophy, 24–5, 31, 60–1

health, 14
Hegel, W. G. F., 71–3, 77
Heidegger, Martin, 35
hermeneutics, 74
heterosexual, 34, 43, 47, 48
history, 71, 72, 73
history, end of, 69

Hobbes, Thomas, 10, 17–19, 20, 29, 30, 37
household, 65
hubris, 58
humanism, 10, 19–20, 32
human nature, 44
human sexuality, *see* sexuality
Husserl, Edmund, 34, 74

ideation, 76
identity, 16, 44, 46, 47–56, 60–6, 70–7, 80, 81, 84
Indian thought, 75
incarnation, 26, 34, 63, 90
individualism, 82
infancy, 70
innovation, 61
interlacing, 21, 46–56
intuition, 60
Islamic extremism, 9

Jesus Christ, 26–9, 90
Judaism, 21, 22–7, 29, 31–4, 38, 57, 62, 64–5, 69, 80
Judeo-Christian, 27, 28

knowledge, 13–14, 18, 28–9, 31, 76, 91
Kojève, Alexanre, 35, 66, 78

language, 70–1, 76
learning theory, 7–8
Leviathan (Hobbes), 30
liberty, 71
life, 14, 18, 69
logic, 71, 72, 77
love, 89–94

Machiavelli, 10, 12, 14–20, 29, 30
Mallarmé, Stéphane, 70–1
male domination, 43
male virility, 40, 55
man/men, 3, 7–9, 11, 13–20, 23–34, 40–4, 58–67, 70–8, 81–8, 90–4
Marx, Karl, 18
masculine, 3, 34, 37–9, 43–5, 48–57, 59–61, 64–5, 70, 73, 77, 80–3, 90
masculine identity, 51–2

mastery, 3, 12, 15–16, 18, 29–32, 40, 55, 76–7, 81
mathematics, 45
maturity, 70, 80, 90
meaning, 76
medicine, 16
memories, 33–4
Messiah, 26
metaphysics, 45, 61
methodology, 41, 69–78
military-industrial complex, 7
millenarianism, 65
mindfulness, 52, 75, 76
moderation, 33, 91
modernity, 32–4, 81–3, 86–8, 90
money, 7
monotheism, 21–4
Montesquieu, 45
morals, 39–45
Moses, 23
mother, 27, 35, 46–8, 50, 59–60, 80
motivations, 8
Muslim, 32
mysogynism, 40

natural rights, 19, 60
natural sciences, 12
nature, 45, 55
   Christianity and, 26–9
   culture and, 58
   getting rid of, 10
   Judaism and, 23–4, 31
   laws of, 59
   mastery of, 3, 15–16, 18, 30–2, 40
   paganism and, 24–5, 31, 58
   relationship with, 2
   state of, 17
non-mastery, 3

obedience, 33
ontogeny, 84
open-mindedness, 3
openness, 55, 64, 76, 77, 80, 91
"other," 48, 52, 53, 63–4, 77, 80

paganism, 3, 21, 24–5, 27–34, 38, 57–65, 69, 72, 80, 90
parousia, 90
perfection, 35, 91
phenomenology, 34, 38
philosopher king, 61
philosophy, 60–1, 70, 71, 73–4, 76, 93–4
phylogenesis, 84
Plato, 17, 58
political authority, 16–17
political sovereignty, 30
politics, 39, 41–4, 57–9, 61, 62, 65–6, 74, 80, 81, 82
polytheism, 21, 22
pornography, 40
power
   Divine, 22, 27
   economic, 9
   over nature, 3, 18, 30–2, 115–16
   state, 7
practice, 70, 79
presence, 89–94
Prince (Machiavelli), 12, 14–17, 18, 30
progressiveness, 66, 82
prostitution, 40
psychoanalysis, 47, 48, 80
psychology, 39, 41–2

realistic, 91
reason, 17
receptiveness, 51, 77
religion, 74
   see also Christianity; Judaism; paganism
Renaissance, 10, 12–16, 19–20, 28, 29, 71
repairing, 79
reproduction, 15–16, 41, 47, 84
responsibility, 23, 89–94
resurrection, 26, 28, 29, 90
Rilke, Rainer Maria, 2
Roman Empire, 24–5

sameness, 52–4, 56
scarcity, 17
science, 11–14, 16, 18, 28
scientific method, 10

secularization, 20, 28–9, 32, 33, 34, 83, 90
self-consciousness, 84, 86, 87, 90, 91
September 11, 2001, 9
sexes, 37–8
  differences between, 42–4, 86
  equality of, 42–3
  relationship between, 45
sexuality
  bi-sexuality, 44, 86, 87
  in childhood, 80
  dual, 44, 77–8
  essential role of, 1, 2, 40, 42
  feminine, 34, 46–56
  globalization and, 2–3, 41
  masculine, 34, 48, 50–6
  nature of, 70
  questioning, 3
  universality of, 41, 42
sociology, 83
Socrates, 60
soul, 60–1
speech, 71
state
  power of, 7
  sovereignty, 17, 30
Stewart, Ian, 45
Strauss, Leo, 18, 32
struggle, 7, 48, 70
subsumption, 27, 31, 58, 65, 69, 90
suicide, 11
survival, 7–9, 17, 18, 29, 47–9, 55, 84
symbol/symbolizing, 3, 8, 9, 11, 15, 25, 32–3, 40, 84, 94
system, 7, 8, 22–3, 25, 78

Taoism, 75, 76, 77, 87, 89, 94
technology, 12
teleology, 52
tension, 3, 8, 14, 23, 32–4, 66, 80–2, 86–8

terrorism, 9, 41, 66
theology, 20, 21–36
theory, 69, 70, 79
thought, 33–4, 75
time, 4, 9, 33, 87–8
  ekstases of, 91
  future-oriented, 69
  globalization and, 75
  lack of, 6, 30, 34–5
  notion of, 65–6
  perception of, 11–12
  theoretical approach to, 69–78
Tocqueville, Alexis de, 88
totalitarianism, 82
tradition, 93
transparency, 30, 31, 91

uncertainty, 8, 91–2
universal, 8, 9, 12, 30, 31, 33, 34, 41–2, 44, 76, 78
utility, 28

violence, 9
virility, 3, 34, 40, 55, 82, 87–8, 90
virilization, 2, 66, 81
virtue, 90

warfare, 41
West, 32, 33, 75, 77
wisdom, 59–60, 72, 80, 94
women, 15–16
  exploitation of, 40
  women's rights, 2, 40–1, 43

Xenophon, 66

yang, 77
yin, 77
youth, 91

CPSIA information can be obtained
at www.ICGtesting.com
Printed in the USA
LVOW08*1835021017
550905LV00005B/131/P